Comments from Readers

52 Things Daughters Need from Th...

"My little girl is almost two and your [...] [...]ctive... It makes you look at who you are, wh[...] you should be, and who you want your daughter to see."

—**Mark, Illinois**

"Two little girls, 10 and 8. I have been thanking God every day for the past week since I saw your book in the airport. Completely inspirational and has driven me to recommit to myself and my family to be a thoughtful and caring presence in their lives."

—**Jim, New York**

"Your book was very touching. I think I even wept at the first few chapters. I am a father to a seven-month-old special girl, and I think it is impossible to do it without God's help. We are on a mission!"

—**Kok Siang, Singapore**

52 Things Kids Need from a Dad

"Your book has inspired me to try harder with my sons and give to them time and wisdom my dad (who wasn't around except for holidays) was unable to give to me."

—**John, Oregon**

"I've highlighted and put notes all over the book, and it's definitely one of my favorites."

—**Aaron, Virginia**

"I have been searching for such a book I can give to my son-in-law as he and my daughter await the birth of their first child...and depending on whether my grandchild is a boy or girl, there may be another book of yours in his future as well!"

—**Bill, California**

52 Things Wives Need from Their Husbands

"Reading your book was a great reminder of simple things I can do to be intentional on a regular basis."

—**Alem, Illinois**

52 Things Husbands Need from Their Wives

"This book is definitely helping me in my marriage as well as my household… For every wife struggling and wondering what's going on in that big head of our husband, I want to say thank you…for your insight, your knowledge, and your suggestions!"

—**Keisha, North Carolina**

52 Things Wives Need from Their Husbands
52 Things Husbands Need from Their Wives

"My husband and I are reading these books together, and it has been so much fun! I love your style of writing. And your words of wisdom have helped me to focus on some things in my marriage I haven't given much thought to for a long time, if ever. You are my new favorite author! Keep up the good work."

—**Rachelle, Wisconsin**

"Thank you for taking the time to share in such a lighthearted, humorous way. Your insights helped us see things from a different perspective. Marriage can be challenging but it is a treasure we must protect."

—**Crystal, Illinois**

10 Conversations Kids Need to Have with Their Dads

"Jay is encouraging to all dads. The '10 conversations' are all important talks we should have with our kids…I still like how he said that the best times to talk to your kids are not always about the important things, but to talk anytime about small things."

—**Mike**

52 Things to PRAY for YOUR KIDS

JAY PAYLEITNER

HARVEST HOUSE PUBLISHERS
EUGENE, OREGON

Cover by Left Coast Design, Portland, Oregon

Cover photo © Chepko Danil Vitalevich

Jay Payleitner is represented by MacGregor Literary, Inc.

52 THINGS TO PRAY FOR YOUR KIDS

Copyright © 2015 by Jay Payleitner
Published by Harvest House Publishers
Eugene, Oregon 97402
www.harvesthousepublishers.com

Library of Congress Cataloging-in-Publication Data
Payleitner, Jay K.
   52 things to pray for your kids / Jay Payleitner.
      pages cm
   ISBN 978-0-7369-6029-8 (pbk.)
   ISBN 978-0-7369-6030-4 (eBook)
   1. Prayer—Christianity. 2. Parents—Prayers and devotions. I. Title. II Title: Fifty-two things to pray for your kids.
   BV283.C5P39 2015
   248.3'2085—dc23

                                                                  2014028432

         14 15 16 17 18 19 20 21 22 23 / VP-JH / 10 9 8 7 6 5 4 3 2 1

Contents

To Rita,
who prays for me.
Keep at it, my love.

A Quiz
Determining your PQ (Prayer Quotient)

Identify the missing word.

1. "Love your enemies and _____ for those who persecute you" (Matthew 5:44).

2. "Very early in the morning, while it was still dark, Jesus got up, left the house and went off to a solitary place, where he _____" (Mark 1:35).

3. "Every Christian needs a half-hour of _____ each day, except when he is busy, then he needs an hour" (Francis de Sales).

4. "Do not be anxious about anything, but in every situation, by _____ and petition, with thanksgiving, present your requests to God" (Philippians 4:6).

5. "Is _____ your steering wheel or your spare tire?" (Corrie Ten Boom)

6. "This, then, is how you should _____: 'Our Father in heaven, hallowed be your name'" (Matthew 6:9).

7. "He who sings, _____ twice" (Augustine).

8. "Watch and _____ so that you will not fall into temptation. The spirit is willing, but the flesh is weak" (Matthew 26:41).

9. "The most promising method of _____ is to allow oneself to be guided by the word of the Scriptures" (Dietrich Bonhoeffer).

10. "_____ without ceasing" (1 Thessalonians 5:17 NASB).

Answers: 1. Pray, 2. Prayed, 3. Prayer, 4. Prayer, 5. Prayer, 6. Pray, 7. Prays, 8. Pray, 9. Prayer, 10. Pray

> *10–9 correct: Prayer Warrior*
> *8–7 correct: Prayer Partner*
> *6–5 correct: Rare Prayer*
> *4 or fewer correct: Needs Prayer*

Foreword

by Nancie Carmichael

What a privilege to meet Jay Payleitner and see the practical, insightful ways he helps parents love their families. Like Jay, my husband and I have come to see that prayer is a powerful way to show the best kind of love to our children.

I am so glad Jay wrote *52 Things to Pray for Your Kids*. In this book, Jay makes the immense calling of praying for our children approachable. We parents know we need to pray for our children, but life just comes at us, and well…we're busy. But Jay offers us practical and realistic ideas on how to pray for our children in the midst of real life. This book is a refreshing reminder to help us see the "prayable" ordinary moments. It's good to know that we don't have to have a certain formula or speak eloquent words. What matters is an honest prayer from our hearts.

As I look back over the years of loving and praying for our five children—each with unique personalities and gifts—I am profoundly grateful for the faithfulness of God in their lives. *Persistent prayer pays.* Now with wonderful in-law children and grandchildren to add to our prayer list, we are privileged to continue the work of prayer for all of them, knowing that prayer is a declaration of our faith as a family. And I'm comforted to know that God answers prayer—not always in the way we think He should, but always faithfully and always for our good. We can trust Him with our dearest treasures.

When I was a little girl, I got out of bed late one night and saw my mother on her knees in front of the living-room couch. She was weeping as she prayed, and I heard her call out her children's names to God. I have never forgotten that holy moment. Now that I am a parent, I understand. My mother is in heaven now, but her prayers held us. They still do. Now we can "pray it forward" for our own children and grandchildren.

In this helpful book, Jay reminds us that prayer is as basic as breathing. Often we parents feel out of control, and let's face it—we *are* out of control. The world is big and scary. Prayer reminds us that God is in control and that prayer is the one thing we can do that will have a profound effect on our children's future. God has a plan and life mission for each of our children. We can't change the world, but we can help shape our children and prayerfully help them see God's best for their lives.

Prayers of faith are powerful prayers. I have learned to pray with thanksgiving. As a parent, it's tempting to pray with worry or fear. Paul encourages us, "Be anxious for nothing, but in everything by prayer and supplication, with thanksgiving, let your requests be made known to God; and the peace of God, which surpasses all understanding, will guard your hearts and minds through Christ Jesus" (Philippians 4:6-7 NKJV). As I thank God for each child, for the work He is doing in them, I experience a sense of peace and relinquishment and faith in my prayers.

God bless you, dear parent, as you remember that Jesus welcomes children—and that He welcomes our prayers. He has the best for our children, and your prayers as a parent, grandparent, or caring relative can change things for eternity. Let Jay's book inspire you to do your most important work ever in praying for your children.

James reminds us, "The prayer of a person living right with God is something powerful to be reckoned with" (James 5:16 MSG).

Nancie Carmichael is the author of *Selah; Lord, Bless My Child*; and many other books. She and her husband, Bill, are the founding publishers of Good Family Magazines, which included *Christian Parenting Today, Virtue,* and *Parents of Teenagers* magazines. nanciecarmichael.c

Introduction:
What a Privilege!

Praying for your kids is not a chore. It's revealing and rewarding. It's exciting. And even amusing.

Got one kid? Two? Three? Every day, set aside three minutes to pray for each of them, and you will quickly discover those three, six, or nine minutes to be the most enjoyable part of your day.

One at a time, picture your children's faces. Imagine what their day might be like. Their bedroom. Their breakfast. Putting on their sandals, sneakers, jellies, boots, or booties. Grabbing their backpack, book bag, or briefcase. Imagine them crawling around your kitchen floor. At preschool. In a classroom. At a workstation. Their interactions with a boss, coach, teacher, boyfriend, or girlfriend. Conversations, questions, assignments, discoveries. Their evening activities—which may be productive or not so productive. Pray God into all those moments.

Don't forget to consider some of the burdens or disappointments they might face this day. Hurt feelings. Unfortunate gossip. Lost friends. Falling short of a goal by one point or one second. Being labeled a failure despite their best effort. Maybe your child is mocked because of something they do—or don't do. Maybe they feel left out because they're homeschooled or have responsibilities other kids don't have. Maybe they're just under a temporary cloud of gloom triggered by a few minor setbacks. Pray God into every moment of their day.

Some of those moments, *you are right there*. You see it all. You laugh with them as they delight in a new discovery. Or they reveal a personal frustration, and you share their heartbreak, lifting a portion of that burden from their shoulders. That interaction is a victory for any mom or dad. Your prayers to have a positive impact on their life have been answered.

But some of those moments *will never be known by you.* In the course of their day, a breathtaking discovery might be made. A painful tribulation might be endured. Sorry, Mom. Sorry, Dad. You won't always be there.

But God is.

That's right. Your regular prayers help connect that child you love so much to the Creator of the universe. And whatever the circumstance, God is going to multiply the joy and divide the grief. Such is the power of prayer.

This book actually doesn't spend much time on the kind of prayers you already do: before meals, tucking in, and when your teenager is driving through a rainstorm. Our deepest desire is to help you see prayer in a new way—as a privilege and an ever present resource. Some chapters will focus on praying *for* your children—whether they're in the next room or miles away. Some chapters should inspire you to spend more time praying *with* your children—modeling how to pray, inviting them to pray, sharing prayer requests as a family. Some chapters are examples of real-life prayers answered in unexpected ways.

One word of caution. (And I speak from experience.) As you pray out loud with your kids, it can be tempting to pretend you're talking to God when in reality your agenda is to instruct or lecture your kids. Have you ever prayed like this?

> *Dear God, keep Bradley safe on the road and help him remember to put on his seat belt and call home when he arrives in Springfield.*

> *Dear God, we pray for Hollywood movie makers to see the value in making more wholesome films and for Whitney not be tempted to go to the midnight showing of* Chainsaw Massacre VII *this Friday.*

Sure, God hears those prayers. And even misdirected prayers that lack sincerity will result in safer kids making better decisions. But much more than that, God wants us to turn to him, trust him, and give glory to him. So when you pray—in the presence of your kids or not—remember who you're talking to.

Okay then. How are you feeling about that idea of intentionally spending three minutes in daily prayer for each of your kids? Is that something you can do? I think it is.

So let's practice. Imagine your newborn, toddler, middle schooler, or college freshman right now. For a moment, set aside the challenges of parenthood. Take a breath and allow the joy of being a mom or dad to wash over you. Make a heart promise to love that child unconditionally. And then go to God. Pray for your son or daughter. By name. Pray expectantly for their today. Pray confidently for their tomorrows. Pray humbly for the role God would have you play in their life.

Then do the same thing tomorrow. And the day after. And the day after. Don't be surprised if you start to pray longer than three minutes. Don't be surprised if you find yourself in communication with God all day, every day on behalf of those kids that God has trusted to your care. What a privilege.

1

Pray When You Hear a Siren

One of the great principles of parenting is the idea that we need to be intentional. Purposeful. Proactive. Our kids need us to anticipate their needs. That's why we plug up electrical outlets before they start to crawl. We play catch with our daughters before they try out for a softball team. We check out the local schools before we buy a house.

In the same way, we should be praying for and with our kids with intentionality. Many of the chapters in this book challenge moms and dads to do things like pray at certain times, for specific character traits, and that specific needs be met.

On the other hand, some of the best parenting moments come when you least expect it. The term *teachable moment* comes to mind. Examples are easy to come by.

- Walking in the woods and seeing poison ivy is when you teach about poison ivy. ("Leaflets three, let it be.")

- When you're watching an innocent TV show and two unmarried folks suddenly jump in the sack, you turn to your middle-schooler and say, "You know that's not how God designed it, right?"

- Taking your kids grocery shopping leads to all kinds of teachable moments: how to pick ripe cantaloupe,

respecting other shoppers, practicing math skills, and why
you shouldn't believe shocking tabloid headlines.

A routine event becomes a connecting point with your kids. Valuable information is transferred from one generation to the next. That's
a teachable moment.

When it comes to prayer, let's teach our kids to look for "prayable
moments."

- You and your little guy or gal are drawing chalk pictures
  on the sidewalk and you hear a siren or several sirens a few
  blocks away. Stop and pray. You don't know details of that
  emergency, but God does.

- You're stuck in a slight traffic jam on the way to school,
  church, a concert, or a sporting event. Turn off the car
  radio and pray that—no matter when you get there—God
  would be honored in the upcoming event. Or pray for
  opportunities for your kids to make a difference today.

- A storm front is moving in. Pray for the safety of your family and your neighbors.

- You pass a church where wedding guests are throwing rice
  at a bride and groom, or you pass a car with a "Just Married" sign. That's a fun prayable moment. Offer a prayer
  for those newlyweds and add a prayer of thanks for your
  own spouse.

- Through social media, radio, TV, or whatever, you find
  out about a breaking national or international news event.
  Whether it's good news or bad news, stop for a moment
  with your kids and express thanks to God that he is in
  control.

Inviting God's involvement in the events of your day—large and
small—is something you probably already do. The Holy Spirit has
given you a sense of discernment that helps you see how God works
continually in the lives of people all around you.

But you may have forgotten to involve your kids. So begin to look for "prayable moments." When you feel called to pray, do it. If your kids are there, even better.

Prayer in the Moment

Heavenly Father. We're not exactly sure how this day will unfold. Within a few miles of us, there are thousands of people with thousands of different needs. It's hard to believe that you are tracking each one. But you are! Thank you for making us mindful of others. Help us respond with love when called. Thank you for being in control of every moment. We pray in the name of your Son, Jesus. Amen.

Before they call I will answer;
while they are still speaking I will hear.

Isaiah 65:24

2

Pray Over Them at Night

You would die for your kids. I know that because I'm a parent just like you, and I would easily give my life for Alec, Randall, Max, Isaac, or Rae Anne. No question about it. I would even trade my life for my daughters-in-law, Lindsay, Rachel, Megan, or Kaitlin. I would especially give my life for my grandsons, Jackson and Judah.

But in the busyness of life, we forget. We're distracted by the ongoing cacophony of the day.

That includes changing diapers, stepping on Happy Meal toys, trying to remember how to do long division, vacuuming trail mix from your car seats, misplacing your smart phone, going out for a gallon of milk at 11:30 at night, worrying about the impact of the casino or strip club opening on the edge of town, signing report cards that could have been better, handing out $20 bills on demand, cleaning baby puke off the shoulder of your favorite jacket, and wondering how hard you should push your kid to make first-chair violin or first-string shortstop.

Okay, so life as moms and dads is filled with challenges, large and small. Still parenthood is a pretty good gig. Those creatures you call children are worth the effort and they will undoubtedly give you a million times more joy than frustration. Kids really are a blessing.

No other relationship has the depth of unconditional and unselfish love that parents have for their children. You choose the person you marry, but they chose you back. There's mutual responsibility. But when you welcome that helpless baby—through birth or adoption—the humbling responsibility of caring for their every need buckles your knees. Nothing can stop you from doing your best for that innocent little gift from God. What a privilege.

Unfortunately, that warm feeling of how awesome it is to be a parent doesn't always wash over you when they're awake. You're just too busy playing zookeeper.

My recommendation (do this right now if you happen to be reading this while the kids are all asleep) is to sneak into every bedroom in your home and say a prayer of gratitude for the blessing God has given you with each son and daughter.

If they're babies, be extra quiet. If they're grade-school age, reach down and touch their warm red cheek. If they're in high school, don't be surprised if they open one eye and mumble, "What are you doing in here?" (Go ahead and tell them that you're praying for them.) If they're away at college, in the military, or finding their own way in the world, stay a little longer and pray extra hard.

There's power when parents pray purposefully for their children. Abraham prayed for Isaac. Hannah prayed for Samuel. David prayed for Solomon. Zacharias prayed for his son, John the Baptist.

And you have to admit, there's something special about prayers in the night. The stillness. The slower pace. The time to consider what really matters.

There's an unspoken bonus when you stop and consider how much love you have for your children. You are getting just a glimpse of how much God loves you. As our heavenly Father, God loves each of us supernaturally and unconditionally. What's more, when God saw that mankind was sinful and had fallen short of his glory, he provided his only Son, Jesus, to pay the price for our sins.

Do you get it? God loves you even more than you love your children.[1]

Prayer for a Grace-Filled Home

Heavenly Father. I delight in the energy of my home. The busyness of my children actually reenergizes me. Watching our kids doing amazing things gives extra purpose and long-range vision to our lives. But children are exhausting and distractions are inevitable, and sometimes I simply forget to pray. Lord, will you tap me on the shoulder a few times every day to lift these kids up to you? I so desperately want your grace to fill every corner of our home. In Jesus' name. Amen.

He said to me, "My grace is sufficient for you, for my power is made perfect in weakness." Therefore I will boast all the more gladly about my weaknesses, so that Christ's power may rest on me.

2 Corinthians 12:9

3

Pray for That Tree House
As You Build It

ike any good dad, I built a tree house in the backyard for my kids. Well, actually it wasn't a tree house. It was more like a stilt house, because although it blended into the tree line at the edge of our property, it wasn't supported by any tree limbs. Well, actually it wasn't a stilt house—it was more like a post house, because there was a single ten-by-ten central post holding up the entire structure. From our kitchen window it looked kind of like a cake box balanced on a stack of soda crackers.

I liked that it looked precarious and swayed in the wind just a bit. But I assure you it was structurally solid. Until it wasn't. Which came four years later.

You see, I had taken great pains to dig a nice big hole and set the specially treated post in an entire wheelbarrow of cement. There was no way that post was going to move. But what I had not figured on was that a harmless looking inch of soil would settle around the base of the post, just above the hardened cement. Over a four-year period, moist soil did what you might expect when it comes into contact with wood. It causes rot. That's not a good thing. Especially when there's a single post supporting the entire tree house. Add the weight of two boys who trusted their dad had built a safe play environment and you've got the formula for potential disaster.

I was actually out of town when 11-year-old Randy and 4-year-old Isaac were goofing around in the soon-to-be-toppled tree house. When Randy realized the whole thing was going down, he heroically picked up his little brother and tossed him onto a nearby tree limb. Randy went down with the slowly collapsing structure. Neither boy was injured, much to the relief of their mom, who witnessed the near disaster from the kitchen window.

The lessons we parents can discover in this unsettling anecdote include quite a few truths. Use wise architectural skills when designing a tree house. Know the principles of wood rot. Dads make mistakes. Employ the buddy system when playing in dangerous surroundings such as your backyard. Moms wish they could, but they can't rescue their kids from every possible dangerous scenario. It's an older brother's job to look out for his little brother.

Another lesson: with your kids, literally walk around your yard and give *practical* real-life instruction on how to use equipment safely and go over the pre-determined house rules.

But the best lesson is this. Along with the previous things, do something else that is *also very practical*. Pray over tree houses. And swing sets. And backyard pools. And sandboxes. And soccer goals. And basketball nets. And horseshoe pits. And trampolines. Ask God to keep your kids and their friends safe while they're in your yard. That's right: we need to consider prayers to be reasonable and practical. It makes sense—it's undeniably logical—to ask the Creator of the Universe to watch over your kids and their pals as they play.

Because—as I found out with that toppling tree house—parents can take every precaution and we still need God to intervene when our best plans fail.

It also helps to have a fearless older brother willing to sacrifice himself to save his little brother. Well done, Randall.

Bonus thought: for heaven's sake, do not allow Jarts or lawn darts of any kind in your backyard. And never leave a kiddie pool unattended. One of the ways God protects children is through the gift of common sense he gave to their parents.

Prayer for Our Backyards

Heavenly Father. Thanks so much for the way you designed kids. To jump and climb and dig in the dirt. To swing high. To bounce even higher. Make this home and yard a welcoming place. And a safe place. Thank you for little cuts and bruises that kids need to experience. Thank you for doctors who can treat broken bones. We pray, heavenly Father, that you keep any child who plays here safe from any serious injuries. We love these children you have given to us. We are amazed to think that you love them even more than we do! We lift our family up to you in the name of your Son, Jesus. Amen.

The name of the Lord is a fortified tower;
the righteous run to it and are safe.

Proverbs 18:10

4

Pray Because Jesus Did

No doubt, moms and dads should model praying for their children. Your kids should regularly see and hear you praying for things big and small. For wisdom and courage. At meals and bedtime. During car trips and before major life events.

When young kids see mom and dad praying, they want to join in. And there's a good chance they'll begin to fashion their own prayers for friends, family members, and people in need. That's fantastic to see.

But as with so many positive character traits, you don't want your children to just mimic you. You want them to own those character traits for themselves. For instance, you want them actually to have good manners, work hard at school, and tell the truth. But it's more important for them to know *why* those things matter. That's why it's a good thing when they ask, "Why?"

Dad and Mom, you'll want to be ready with answers that make sense. "Good manners are important because they show respect for other people—people loved by God." "You should work hard at school because you are responsible for developing the gifts given to you by the Creator." "Telling the truth is important because God is Truth and we're made in his image."

So how do you answer the question, "Why do we pray?"

Of course, it's not just to ask for stuff. And it's not to show how holy we are. It's also not to inform God of our needs or desires. That's stuff he already knows.

So here are three really good answers.

1. We pray to know God better. Just like talking to anyone we care about.

2. We pray to know his plan for us. Because it's a good one.

3. We pray to glorify him in our lives and affirm our dependence on him.

But perhaps the best proof that prayer is valuable and necessary is that Jesus prayed. He prayed often. And he prayed in different places, for different things, and for different reasons. For example, Jesus prayed alone.

> *Very early in the morning, while it was still dark, Jesus got up, left the house and went off to a solitary place, where he prayed (Mark 1:35).*

He prayed with others.

> *Those present were Peter, John, James and Andrew; Philip and Thomas, Bartholomew and Matthew; James son of Alphaeus and Simon the Zealot, and Judas son of James. They all joined together constantly in prayer, along with the women and Mary the mother of Jesus, and with his brothers (Acts 1:13-14).*

Jesus prayed for hours at a time.

> *One of those days Jesus went out to a mountainside to pray, and spent the night praying to God (Luke 6:12).*

Jesus prayed for the faith of others.

> *"I have prayed for you, Simon, that your faith may not fail. And when you have turned back, strengthen your brothers" (Luke 22:32).*

He prayed for routine needs.

> *"Give us today our daily bread" (Matthew 6:11).*

After raising Lazarus from the dead, Jesus prayed in gratitude for answered prayers.

> *They took away the stone. Then Jesus looked up and said, "Father, I thank you that you have heard me. I knew that you always hear me, but I said this for the benefit of the people standing here, that they may believe that you sent me" (John 11:41-42).*

In the Garden of Gethsemane, Jesus also demonstrated how to pray in desperate times. Even though he was fully aware that his prayer might not be answered in the way he hoped.

> *He withdrew about a stone's throw beyond them, knelt down and prayed, "Father, if you are willing, take this cup from me; yet not my will, but yours be done." An angel from heaven appeared to him and strengthened him. And being in anguish, he prayed more earnestly, and his sweat was like drops of blood falling to the ground (Luke 22:41-44).*

Mom and Dad, will you be ready when your children ask, "Why should I pray?"

Prayer for Our Children's Prayer Life

Heavenly Father. We are so privileged to come to you in prayer. To be able to talk to you and bring our needs, fears, and failures to you. Help us as parents to come to you often for guidance. Help our children come to you without hesitation. Help us to pray like Jesus. Consistently. Humbly. In gratitude. In desperation. We know that prayer is a pathway to know you and your will for our lives. Thank you for listening to us and caring about us as individuals. In the name of Jesus, I pray. Amen.

Jesus said, "Let the little children come to me, and do not hinder them, for the kingdom of heaven belongs to such as these."

Matthew 19:14

5

Pray for Their Future Spouse

One of the most surreal experiences for any parent is praying for your son's future wife or your daughter's future husband. You're praying for an individual you can't identify and haven't yet met. (All four of my sons met their future wives after college.)

Or maybe you already know that future son- or daughter-in-law, but the match isn't going to be made for a decade. Your ten-year-old daughter might one day marry her older brother's best friend. The bratty little girl down the street could grow into a gracious beauty that catches your son's eye.

Have you ever videotaped a middle-school choir concert? Most of the time, you focus on your own kid. But I always made sure to include a panning shot of the entire choir just in case a future son- or daughter-in-law was also on those risers.

When my son Randall announced he was beginning to court a lovely red-haired girl who was the friend of a friend, we wanted to know all about her. Randall said, "You met her last summer at the pool party." Still, we couldn't picture the girl named Rachel. Then I remembered how I had asked all twenty guests that day to casually pose for quick photos in groups of two or three. We already had a photo of our future daughter-in-law and I didn't even know it! For some reason, it's easier to pray for someone when you can picture them in your head.

Moms and dads, praying for your child's future spouse can lead to real blessings. Plus it's a fun, thought-provoking, and revealing activity.

It really does help to contemplate the future with your kids, especially before they begin any real interest in the opposite sex. They're not dating, so you're not thinking of specific boyfriends or girlfriends. Praying for your child's future spouse helps you see your child as a person you are preparing for the future. Not just their career, but the more important task of equipping them for meaningful adult relationships. Part of your job is to teach them how to love, forgive, listen, care, be tender, be tough, sacrifice, and put the needs of other before themselves.

When you pray for a future spouse, you're laying the foundation for your son to be a godly husband or your daughter to be a godly wife, if God calls them to be married. Which is an interesting point. That child you're praying for may be called to singleness. And that has to be okay.

Paul remained single and saw it as a gift. In 1 Corinthians 7:7-8, he takes a moment from his instructions to married people to give a sincere shout-out to individuals who are called to singleness: "I wish that all of you were as I am. But each of you has your own gift from God; one has this gift, another has that. Now to the unmarried and the widows I say: It is good for them to stay unmarried, as I do."

As my boys announced their engagements, Rita and I had the delightful privilege to tell Lindsay, Rachel, Megan, and Kaitlin that we had been praying for them for years. Not praying that our sons would each find a wife. We were praying for *them*. As individuals. Rita and I prayed that God would protect these girls as they grew into young women and prepare their hearts to be united with our sons.

Like so many prayers in this book, this is one you can pray on your own in private, with your spouse, and with your child. But be careful not to put expectations on your son or daughter. They don't have to get married. And they certainly don't have to marry the first boy or girl that catches their eye. Have lots of conversations about love, marriage, sex, and what to look for in a spouse. And make it a point to close those conversations with prayer. Pray your child hears, understands, and surrenders to God's will. Pray for God's protection on that boy or girl who *may* be out there, who God *may* be preparing to be a lifelong marriage partner for your son or daughter.

While you're at it, pray for the marriages of all the couples you know.

Pray for your own marriage. And pray that you and your spouse will be welcoming and loving in-laws to that future new member of your family.

Prayer for Someone You Don't Know Yet

Heavenly Father. Because you see all of the past and all of the future, you may even see a day when Logan watches a beautiful girl in a white dress walk down the aisle of a church to become his bride. Since he's only in third grade, that's a long time away. But if marriage is part of your plan for Logan, we want to pray for that day and that girl. She may live in a different state or different country even. Or she may be a classmate of Logan's right now! Wherever she is, protect her. And love her. And draw her to you. And when that right girl comes along, please make it very clear to our son. And Lord, bless our family and thank you for the marriage you've given to me. We honor your design for families. In the name of your Son, Jesus. Amen.

He who finds a wife finds what is good
and receives favor from the Lord.

Proverbs 18:22

6

Pray Watching the Horizon

If you've been watching your son or daughter play an outdoor sport for more than a few years, you've experienced this. You're walking from the parking lot toward the playing field—soccer, baseball, softball, lacrosse, field hockey, track, football—and you're still more than a hundred yards away. The entire team is warming up. You can't see uniform numbers. You can't see faces. From that distance, there's no way anyone could possibly distinguish one player from another.

But you can. You know your kid. The way they jog, the way they stand, the way they interact with their teammates. Your memory and their silhouette match. And you smile. That's your kid, and it doesn't matter if they play every minute or ride the bench the entire game, your love runs deep and your commitment is absolute.

Of course, you just saw them this morning. You told them you were looking forward to the game and would try to get to the field on time. Seeing them was not exactly a surprise.

Now consider a scene described by Jesus in one of his best-known parables. You know the story. But you may not have thought too much about that moment when the father of the prodigal son saw the unmistakable figure of his youngest boy approaching from a distance. Here's how Jesus begins the parable:

> *"A man had two sons. The younger son told his father, 'I want*

*my share of your estate now before you die.' So his father agreed
to divide his wealth between his sons.*

*"A few days later this younger son packed all his belongings and
moved to a distant land, and there he wasted all his money in
wild living. About the time his money ran out, a great famine
swept over the land, and he began to starve. He persuaded a
local farmer to hire him, and the man sent him into his fields
to feed the pigs. The young man became so hungry that even
the pods he was feeding the pigs looked good to him. But no
one gave him anything.*

*"When he finally came to his senses, he said to himself, 'At home
even the hired servants have food enough to spare, and here
I am dying of hunger! I will go home to my father and say,
"Father, I have sinned against both heaven and you, and I am
no longer worthy of being called your son. Please take me on
as a hired servant."' So he returned home to his father" (Luke
15:11-20 NLT).*

Consider what that father has been doing for all those months. He
may have been upset when the younger son insisted on an early share
of his inheritance. But any anger didn't last long. He loved the boy and
spent some time worrying about him. Plus, he had to make sure the
older son—who now had twice as much work to do—still felt appreciated. And don't forget, famine had swept the country and he was probably busy trying to minimize crop losses.

Through all that he kept an eye on the horizon. Surely he prayed.
And watched for any sign of that familiar silhouette walking down
that dusty road. When he saw the boy, what did he do? Did he turn
his back and force the boy to grovel? Did he fold his arms and prepare
to deliver a long lecture? That father did what you would do. He ran.
With arms wide open.

*"And while he was still a long way off, his father saw him
coming. Filled with love and compassion, he ran to his son,
embraced him, and kissed him. His son said to him, 'Father, I*

have sinned against both heaven and you, and I am no longer worthy of being called your son.'

"But his father said to the servants, 'Quick! Bring the finest robe in the house and put it on him. Get a ring for his finger and sandals for his feet. And kill the calf we have been fattening. We must celebrate with a feast, for this son of mine was dead and has now returned to life. He was lost, but now he is found.' So the party began" (Luke 15:20-24).

Jesus finishes the story with an emotional and instructive conversation between the father and the older son. The theological connotations of the parable are profound. The master teacher was providing a graphic image of God's unconditional love and confirming that no matter what you've done, God will always celebrate the day when you finally surrender to grace.

That's a huge lesson. Really, that's the entire point of the Bible, isn't it? But you're still thinking about that kid walking over the hill and his dad coming out with a big old bear hug.

Mom and Dad, when your children leave home—for a school day, a summer mission trip, a college semester, a tour of duty, or some "wild living"—don't ever lose sight of the horizon. Keep watching expectantly. You can do that because you've made your home a place your offspring are always welcome. Pray they feel your unconditional love. Pray for their safe return. Pray for your own open arms and open heart.

The father's response throughout the entire story reminds us to be patient with our children. They are going to disappoint you. They may turn their back on you. They may squander your hard-earned money on stuff you don't approve of. The example of the prodigal's father models how we need to watch and wait expectantly. When you first get a glimpse of that son or daughter you know so well and love so much, run to them. And get ready to party.

Prayer for Prodigals

Heavenly Father. So much of what we need to do as parents, you have already modeled for us. Your generosity. Allowing us to make our own decisions. Forgiving us. Instructing us. Your unconditional love. As parents, help us do all those things. And when our children choose wild living or end up in disturbing situations like eating with pigs, protect them. Keep us filled with patience and hope. And we look forward to the ultimate party with you and all our children in your perfect timing. We pray in the name of Jesus. Amen.

The Lord is compassionate and gracious,
  slow to anger, abounding in love.
He will not always accuse,
  nor will he harbor his anger forever;
he does not treat us as our sins deserve
  or repay us according to our iniquities.

Psalm 103:8-10

7

Pray They Get Caught

For years, Ben and Sarah routinely said a prayer they hoped would not come true for any of their four children. They knew how kids could be. They knew how the culture pulls good kids from good homes to make not-so-good decisions. My friend Ben is especially aware because he was more than a bit rebellious in his younger days. Looking at him, you wouldn't know it today, but Ben was deep into narcotics in his early twenties.

So Ben and Sarah prayed specifically that if and when their children did something illegal or immoral or simply made a really bad choice, they would get caught.

Those are the exact words they used. And not long ago their prayer was answered. It was a holiday weekend with lots of activity in the house, and Sarah needed something that had last been seen in their teenage daughter's closet. Looking there, she found a bottle of rum and some fruit-mixer concoction.

The Christmas celebration took a sharp, unpleasant, yet necessary turn. With sincere apologies, some of the guests were asked to leave. The festivities were postponed. The family huddled and their daughter was confronted.

I wasn't there, so I don't know exactly what was said. But the core message was very personal and very compelling. Up until that day, Ben's four children had only had an inkling of their father's drug addiction from two decades earlier. How far he'd fallen. And how God had rescued him. It wasn't a pleasant story. And it's not a story you should tell to small children. After all, when kids are young and impressionable, they need to see dad as a hero. Invincible. A solid rock they can count on.

Ben had been that dependable dad for their entire lives. Which is a great thing. And which made his testimony to his children even more powerful. Over the years, he had shared his story with men's groups and other individuals who were struggling with addiction. He talked about Satan's power, hitting bottom, and finding hope only after turning his life over to Christ. But his kids only knew small bits and pieces of the story.

That evening they heard something they didn't want to hear but needed to. However, they were old enough to listen, understand, and learn from their father's mistakes. The teenager who was hiding the liquor really didn't receive a severe punishment. Listening to her dad open up about his personal battle—the stumbling, helplessness, surrender, and recovery—had more than enough impact. In a sense, the family was broken that night. But they soon healed stronger than ever.

Thinking about Ben and Sarah, the word that comes to mind is *courage*. Courage to overcome. Courage to trust. Courage to pray the way they did for their kids. And courage to see the big picture. They weren't just dealing with a bottle of rum found in a teenager's closet. They were standing up against Satan, who had chosen that Christmas season to try to seize a new foothold in their family. But he didn't have a chance. Instead of sweeping it under the rug or delaying any repercussions until after the family event, that mom and dad addressed the situation firmly, efficiently, and without hesitation. How did they know what to do and what to say? Only because that's what they had been praying for.

Your past may be different than Ben's. But your children are facing the same cultural challenges. Do you have the courage to pray for your children to get caught? Will you have the courage to confront your children's unhealthy choices at the top of the slippery slope?

Prayer for Wise Choices for Kids and Parents

Heavenly Father. We pray that our kids make choices that honor you. But we also know they have sinned and will sin. In their humanness, they will fall short of your glory. In humility and brokenness, we ask that you open our eyes to those times we need to intervene. We pray they get caught. In those difficult moments, we pray that we have the courage and wisdom to respond with love and truth. And, thank you for preparing our hearts and minds so we can be the parents our children need in every situation. In times of joy. And in times when the world seems to be crumbling around us. Thank you for being our rock. We love and trust you. In Jesus' name. Amen.

Pray that we may be delivered from wicked and evil people, for not everyone has faith. But the Lord is faithful, and he will strengthen you and protect you from the evil one.

2 Thessalonians 3:2-3

8

Pray Psalm 127

It's only five verses. But it provides a warning, a reminder, a promise, a key image on which every parent should meditate, and an endorsement for having lots of kids.

Let's read it together. Even better, stop right now, go find your kids, and read it with them.

> *Unless the LORD builds a house,*
> *the work of the builders is wasted.*
> *Unless the LORD protects a city,*
> *guarding it with sentries will do no good.*
> *It is useless for you to work so hard*
> *from early morning until late at night,*
> *anxiously working for food to eat;*
> *for God gives rest to his loved ones.*
> *Children are a gift from the LORD;*
> *they are a reward from him.*
> *Children born to a young man*
> *are like arrows in a warrior's hands.*
> *How joyful is the man whose quiver is full of them!*
> *He will not be put to shame when he confronts his accusers at*
> *the city gates.*
>
> *Psalm 127 NLT*

The warning. A home without God is not a home at all. It's a collection of people who happen to be related to each other living under the same roof. A community that turns its back on God is vulnerable to attack by the dark forces of the world. If you invite him, the Lord will build your home. The Lord will protect your city.

The reminder. Fifty times per year, we need to put in a good solid week of work and then trust God to provide. What good is a home if you are never home? If your job pulls you away from your family and you still have anxiety about providing for them, then something has to change. Consider a new job. A smaller house. Different career goals. Also, start to apply the fourth commandment to your life. The idea of setting aside one day a week to recharge and reprioritize is a pretty solid strategy.

The promise. Kids are not a burden. They're a blessing. A reward. Expect joy and you just may get it!

The key image. My original thought was that the image of a warrior is mostly for dads. But I've known enough moms who have fiercely protected and fought for their kids that I've expanded my view. Our kids need mothers and fathers to work together to prepare every member of the family for battle. To sharpen our arrows. To hone them straight and true. To help each child find just the right target matching their skills and giftedness. To hold them close to our heart. And let them fly. When you're feeling powerless, meditate on the image of the steadfast archer. That's God's design for parents.

The endorsement. How full is your quiver? I'm on record endorsing big families. And in Psalm 127, God does too! Good moms and dads (like you) who raise responsible kids should welcome babies into their home through birth, adoption, fostering, or even taking in nieces, nephews, or grandkids who need a secure foundation for a season of life. I totally understand there are all kinds of reasons why one or two children (or none) might be the right amount for some families. But don't stop having children because you can't afford it or because you've heard the earth is too crowded. God promises his provision. And I have the sense the kids growing up in your home will not be adding to the problems of the world—they will be part of the solution. By the way, according to the last words of this psalm, when the mayor and other city officials get together, they will be saying nice things about that big family of yours.

It's only five verses. Pray it with your kids every night for two weeks and you'll all have it memorized. Then do the same thing in a couple months with the twenty-third psalm. It's a good one too.

Prayer of a Steadfast Warrior

Heavenly Father. I accept the role of warrior and protector for my family. Help me sharpen my arrows and prepare myself and prepare them for battle. As you challenge us in Ephesians chapter 6, we want to live by your strength and power. Remind each member of my family to put on the belt of truth, breastplate of righteousness, shield of faith, helmet of salvation, and sword of the Spirit. Prepare our feet to run and spread the good news. And even to run to the battle. Help us be fearless for you. In Jesus' name. Amen.

Blessed are all who fear the LORD,
who walk in obedience to him.
You will eat the fruit of your labor;
blessings and prosperity will be yours.
Your wife will be like a fruitful vine
within your house;
your children will be like olive shoots
around your table.
Yes, this will be the blessing
for the man who fears the LORD.

Psalm 128:1-4

9

Pray for Their Teams
and Teammates

Yeah, we did traveling club sports. With five kids who enjoyed competition, Rita and I drove all over the Midwest for wrestling, soccer, baseball, and softball. Plus, during their middle school and high school careers we sat in bleachers for all those sports plus football, basketball, volleyball, and track.

For sure, we endured devastating losses and spectacular victories. On some teams our offspring rode the bench and saw minimal playing time. Other times they were MVPs.

Looking back, some of our proudest moments came at the end-of-the-year banquets. Coaches made speeches and gave out awards. Athletes dressed up in semiformal attire (almost unrecognizable out of their sweaty uniforms). Whether it was a winning season or not, parents celebrated the young men and women who seemed to be growing up right before our eyes.

But it wasn't any award, dramatic video, or personal accolades that were the highlight of those evenings for Rita and me. Season after season, in several sports, with all five of my children, the coach would ask a Payleitner from their team to say grace before the meal.

It wasn't something my children would have asked to do. But somehow…perhaps a dozen different coaches knew that the team member with the name Payleitner on their jersey would feel comfortable and courageous enough to say a short prayer before releasing the gathered crowd to line up and fill our paper plates with mostaccioli, baked chicken, sloppy joes, or whatever was waiting in long aluminum pans on long wobbly tables.

To be clear, these were public-school, city, or park district teams. Prayer was hardly mandatory. As a matter of fact, in some regions of our great country, prayer at events like this might be considered scandalous. Many of those in attendance probably didn't even pray at home before meals. But those coaches knew that Alec, Randy, Max, Isaac, or Rae Anne was the right person to ask. And I could not have been more proud and felt more humble watching my son or daughter respectfully and efficiently ask God to bless these meals.

Rita and I probably took it for granted. Actually, we came to expect it. But as I think about it now, the fact that our kids were given that honor is quite a statement. Our kids had earned the respect of their coaches and were vocal enough about their personal convictions that it must have been the easy and obvious choice.

A couple of other thoughts come to mind. The coaches always asked our kids ahead of time, but Rita and I usually didn't know about it until they stepped up to the podium. Also, we almost never asked, "Why did the coach pick you?" The one or two times we did ask, the answer was, "It's not a big deal. He knew I would say yes."

Here's the point. I can't imagine any of my kids preaching the gospel in the dugout or locker room. But I can imagine them promising a teammate they'd pray for a sick mom. Or quietly mentioning to a teammate how they worked out a problem with God's help. I can also confirm that some juvenile shenanigans were toned down because one of my kids said something like, "We could do that. But we need to wrap it up by midnight. And no eggs and no spray paint."

My five kids were no angels, but in general they proved to have a positive influence on their teammates. Years later, one mother told us, "When my son went out, I always knew that if Max was along, the boys wouldn't get in any trouble." Considering the environment of most public high schools in America, that's high praise.

Any time your kids are part of a group, the situation deserves several layers of prayer. And that might be different for each one of your children. As groupthink begins to take over, pray for your child's own personal wisdom and discernment, and pray for his or her leadership and influence. Perhaps pray that they may have the opportunity to lead a teammate to faith in Christ. Also, pray for the other members of the team, class, club, or group. Pray for their safety, team camaraderie, sportsmanship, and so on. As individuals, pray that their hearts are not hardened to God at work in their lives, and pray that they see your child as a positive influence.

While you're at it, you might ask God to help you be a good role model and positive force in the bleachers, with other parents, and with coaches.

Prayer for Being a Team Player

Heavenly Father. Thank you for the many gifts you've given Ethan. What a blast it is to watch him on the soccer field. There's no way we can know every other boy on the team and what's going on in their world. We know that emotions run high during games and practices. Lord, we can't be there. But you can. Please help Ethan honor you when he's with his teammates and coaches. Help him reflect your love and grace with his words and actions even during high-pressure moments. In locker rooms, on the team bus, at school, and when the team gets together, please protect Ethan and all the boys. We love and trust you. In Jesus' name. Amen.

"This is to my Father's glory, that you bear much fruit, showing yourselves to be my disciples."

Jesus, in John 15:8

10

Pray That Their Eyes Be Opened

Over a period of several years, we welcomed ten foster babies into our home. Mostly newborns. Some had been abandoned in the hospital. Some had health issues that were overwhelming for the birth mother. And some were cocaine-exposed. That means the mother had been doing drugs while she was pregnant and her baby was, essentially, born addicted to cocaine. Which meant the innocent newborn was in line for some nasty withdrawal symptoms.

I will never forget my son Max holding one of those precious babies while she was experiencing severe withdrawal tremors. You have to understand this was right around the time he was an all-conference fullback, state-qualifying wrestler, and starting catcher for the baseball team that placed fourth in the state. He was a tough kid with a high threshold for pain.

When Max realized what that innocent baby was going through, he held her tight and close just as he had seen his mom doing. After the tremors subsided, Max calmly handed the baby to Rita and then he let loose his own physical and emotional response to what he had just experienced. With justifiable anger, Max said, "How could a mother do this to her baby?"

Max was never on a path to drug or alcohol abuse, but you can imagine how holding that helpless baby in the throes of a seizure was a wake-up call to the hopelessness and waste of life that comes from addictive behaviors.

Rita and I didn't get involved with foster care to teach our kids about the dangers of substance abuse. But we did pray for our children to grow healthy and learn to make wise decisions. That's how God works—often using parents to provide opportunities through which children can make their own discoveries about good and bad decisions.

We parents grit our teeth on an amusement-park roller coaster, but it's worth it when our eight-year-old says, "Phew. I'm glad I had my seat belt on."

At a group picnic there might be an entire table filled with cupcakes and brownies, but we don't always give long lectures on eating sensibly. After all, it's a picnic! When your fourth-grader doesn't feel so good after six trips to the sweets table, all you have to say is, "Might it be something you ate?"

We invite our middle-schooler along to help deliver diapers and baby clothes to a pregnancy resource center so they can see firsthand the challenges of teen motherhood.

So keep praying that your kids learn to make wise decisions. But remember, the best way to open their eyes to right and wrong is often through direct personal experience. That includes discovering on their own that it's a good decision to stay away from drugs, wear seat belts, eat sensibly, and save sex for marriage.

Mom and Dad, spend time with your kids—holding babies, going to amusement parks and picnics, volunteering for real-life ministries. You just might get a chance to see your prayers answered in very specific ways.

Prayer for Wise Decision Making

Heavenly Father. Over the course of her life, Emma will be making millions of decisions. Most are not really a big deal. Like what socks to wear. Or whether to get rocky road or mint chocolate chip. But some decisions are huge. Lord, we know one of the reason you designed parents was to teach our kids how to make wise decisions. And we promise to do the best we can. But we're asking you to help Emma as only you can. Teach her things we can't. Teach her things that parents sometimes don't think about. Open her eyes to make discoveries about how your world works. And how she can serve you best. As she's learning, Emma will surely make a few mistakes. Please protect her along the way. We love and trust you. In Jesus' name. Amen.

Once more Jesus put his hands on the man's eyes. Then his eyes were opened, his sight was restored, and he saw everything clearly.

Mark 8:25

11

Pray for Daily Bread

A friend of mine spent a summer of his youth working on a wheat farm. Fifteen years later, that experience turned into an extraordinary and ongoing prayer event for him and his children.

Typically, Scott would take a moment before bedtime prayers with his two sons and ask about their day and then allow that conversation to flow naturally into specific prayers of gratitude and provision. But one night he was tired and distracted, so instead of initiating a dialogue and praying spontaneously, he simply launched into the Lord's Prayer.

When he got to "give us this day our daily bread," a light went on in his head and he began to laugh out loud. His two boys were a bit confused. After a moment, Scott turned to his two sons and said, "Do you have any idea what it takes for God to supply us with our daily bread?" One of the boys wisecracked, "Well, he doesn't go to the store."

Scott wisely ignored the joke and plowed into a lesson those boys will never forget. He explained that there were a million steps before a slice of bread gets spread with peanut butter and jelly for lunch. Before the twist-tie is untwisted. Before the loaf of bread wrapped in plastic even makes it to the store. And then he ran through just a few of the steps it took for his sons to get their daily slices of bread.

Test the soil for mineral content. Till the soil. With a wheat drill, spread the seeds. Pray for rain, but not too much rain. Weed. Watch for rusts, blights, smuts, and lodging. When moisture content is between

12 and 13 percent, harvest. Cut, thresh, store. Kill the weevils, mites, and psocids. Protect from rats. Retain a percentage of seed for next year. Ship the grain to a gristmill.

That was just the first night of prayer, because those are the steps of bread making that are performed at the wheat farm. And that's really all that Scott knew. The boys never even knew that their dad had spent a summer working on a farm. They were amused and amazed at the thought of their dad hanging out with tractors and shoveling grain into bins and bags. Suddenly, eating their daily bread took on a new dimension.

So Scott did a little research.

A few nights later, that dad picked up where he left off. After the wheat leaves the farm, he explained, the process continues.

Separate the endosperm from the bran and germ. Grind and sack the flour. Ship to bakeries. Add just the right amount of yeast (and all those other ingredients). Rise, bake, slice, bag. Twist-tie closed. Haul bread. Monitor for freshness. Stack on shelves. Transfer to shopping cart (with or without wobbly wheels). Check out. Make sure bag boy doesn't put bread in bottom of bag. Plop loaf on kitchen counter. Twist-tie open. Pull out a fresh slice. Spread with PB&J. Eat.

The boys had never thought about it before. Unless it's part of your daily grind, most people don't. But when we do stop and consider the process, it's quite humbling. At every phase there are a dozen things that could go wrong. From planting too deep to toasting too dark. During dozens of prayer times and conversations, Scott found himself talking about God's provision and protection.

He also found that the life cycle of a simple stalk of grain is a word picture used frequently in Scripture. It seemed like every time he opened his Bible he found another story or metaphor he could share with his boys. Sow in good soil. Only when a kernel dies can it produce fruit. From small beginnings comes significant harvest. Seasons change. You reap what you sow. Wheat and weeds may grow side by side but have different destinations. The harvest takes work...and workers. Man does not live by bread alone.

It turns out a loaf of bread is a profound reminder of God's generous and consistent provision. Next time you find yourself reciting the Lord's Prayer or eating a peanut-butter-and-jelly sandwich with your kids, go ahead and stop and ask, "How does God provide our daily bread?"

Oh yeah, don't ever again complain about paying four bucks for a good loaf of bread.

Prayer for Provision

Heavenly Father. We are amazed at your generosity. How you supply all our needs. And yet sometimes we forget. We think it's our hard work that somehow earns the food on our table and roof over our head. But it's all you. It's your morning sun we wake to. It's your air we breathe. It's your fields and livestock that feed us. It's your working through us that allows us to make a living. It's all you. No doubt, it's all you. Yes, Lord. Give us this day our daily bread. It's really more than we deserve. But you love us and we trust you with all our needs. In Jesus' name. Amen.

"Which of you, if your son asks for bread, will give him a stone? Or if he asks for a fish, will give him a snake? If you, then, though you are evil, know how to give good gifts to your children, how much more will your Father in heaven give good gifts to those who ask him!"

Jesus, in Matthew 7:9-11

12

Pray Rocking

Rita and I have five kids. And each birth was different.

When you're expecting, your prayers tend to be for the very near future. For healthy pregnancies and surprise-free deliveries. Well, one of our babies came six weeks early; we had one emergency C-section, one C-section during which the epidural didn't take, and a VBA3C. (If you don't know what that is, do an online search.) Two of the boys ended up in a high-risk neonatal intensive care unit for a couple of weeks. So we did have some surprises, but all five came home strong and healthy.

Let me quickly clarify. I said "we had" all those things. It was the amazing Rita who "had" all those things. I was there. But really, all I did was fetch ice chips and snap some interesting photos. And I didn't faint.

When you're holding a newborn, your prayers still don't reach too far into the future. Leaving the maternity ward you're still in a kind of new-parent daze, so the urgency of the here-and-now becomes your focus. The welcome-home moments for Alec, Randall, Maximilian, Isaac, and Rae Anne were also all very different. When Alec came home, it was two young kids bringing home their own kid to an empty rental house. Rae Anne came home to four older brothers who held her, poked her, and didn't always keep the noise down.

All that happened over a 15-year span. In that time, we did lose one baby to a first-trimester miscarriage. I don't think of that loss very often, but Rita does once in a while. Prayer saw us through that challenging season as well.

Once newborns get home, a mom and dad's next round of prayers are filled with gratitude and humility that God would give them such a profound responsibility. It can be more than a little overwhelming. Then, after that surge of emotional connection with God, the familiar rhythms of your old life settle back in. Work. Sleep. Play. Eat. Church. Shop. Clean. Pay bills. Date night. Visit relatives. Coordinate calendars. Romance. And so on. In and through those rituals of life lies the danger that prayer becomes routine.

But now with a newborn you add an entire new list of things that may throw off those rhythms. Things like changing diapers, midnight feedings, and rocking your baby to sleep.

And that is the turning point in the prayer life of every parent.

Rocking an infant is often the time when new parents—especially first-time parents—begin to balance two kinds of prayers. Prayers for the moment. And prayers for the future.

You look down and see that perfect specimen of humanity. (Even if that little one is not perfect according to the health professionals.) And you pray they sleep soundly. You pray that the dog, the doorbell, the siblings don't wake them. You pray that the diaper doesn't leak through. And you pray a moment of rest for yourself.

Simultaneously, you give yourself permission to pray for their future. It's a daring undertaking. You pray they find their place in this world, make friends, learn to love, find a worthy husband or wife, and accept Christ into their lives at an early age. You may even pray that your little one gets so proficient at life that someday they don't need you anymore. Those are all rocking-chair prayers.

When you are not in that chair, life may explode again. Away from the rocking chair you do the silly things that all parents do. You worry about their hairline. You sterilize their pacifier way too often (at least with the first one or two babies). You post daily photos online and base your self-esteem on the quantity of likes and comments. Worst of all, you start comparing your child to those frustrating developmental benchmarks. When they roll from tummy to back a week before the national norm, you begin to imagine you're raising an Olympic athlete. When they don't play peek-a-boo by a certain age, you start contacting tutors so they don't fall further behind.

My recommendation for parents with kids of any age: go back to the rocking chair. When they don't fit on your lap any more, move to an overstuffed chair. And then a sofa. If your teenager falls asleep with their head on your lap or shoulder, just keep praying. Pray for the moment. Pray for the future.

And, oh yeah. If you don't have a rocking chair, then beg, borrow, buy, or steal one today.

Prayer for Perspective

Heavenly Father. Let me rest in you. Let me slow down on a regular basis in order to pray deeply and surrender to your will. Allow me to physically connect with Anna and Evan so I can spiritually connect with you. I know I can never have your vision. But give me the perspective to see past today. A glimpse of the future would go a long way toward getting through the grind of the present. Still, I trust you. Thank you also for the home you've given us. And all the special places where I can rock, hug, and snuggle with my babies. Even when they're about to graduate high school. I pray in the name of your Son, Jesus. Amen.

Godliness is profitable for all things, since it holds
promise for the present life and also for the life to come.

1 Timothy 4:8 NASB

13

Pray for Angels

You don't have to believe all the stories you hear of angels. But you have to believe some of them. Angels are real. And it might be a good idea to thank God for their presence and involvement in our lives.

One grown woman vividly recalls the day her mom dropped her off at school back in sixth grade. They were running late and had parked across the street from their normal drop-off zone. The distracted girl had stepped into traffic, when she was lifted off the ground and pulled back to the car. The woman describes the feeling as having a slow-motion quality…as a pickup truck whooshed by inches in front of her. When she turned breathlessly to thank her mother for pulling her to safety, she realized her mom had watched the entire scene unfold from much too far away to have reached her in time. The heroic hand that saved her life was not from this world. The scene sounds like something described in Psalm 91:11-12: "He will command his angels concerning you to guard you in all your ways; they will lift you up in their hands."

A mother and father nod to the hospital chaplain who joins them in silent prayer at the bedside of their son, who's barely clinging to life. They expect the chaplain to offer a few obligatory prayers and move to the next room. Instead, still without speaking, the older gentleman sits with the couple in vigil for the entire night. When the sun comes up, a flurry of doctors and nurses hustle in and out of the room as the boy comes out of his coma. Only when things settle down do the parents attempt to find the chaplain who sat, prayed, and ushered a quiet strength into the room. The nurse in charge assures them that there was no chaplain on duty that night. The entire family turns their life over to God, realizing they were visited by an angel. Which is entirely possible. After all, Hebrews 1:14 says, "Are not all angels ministering spirits sent to serve those who will inherit salvation?"

Some of the stories of hero angels, of course, can be explained in human terms. But there are enough stories around shared by thoughtful, even formerly skeptical, individuals that you can be quite sure angels move in and out of our lives on a regular basis. The small child lost for days in a national park—protected and led to safety by a "nice man dressed in white." In a dark alley, thugs retreat from their assault because two massive dudes unexpectedly show up right behind the intended victim. A stranger pulls an accident victim out of a burning car but disappears before paramedics arrive.

Some church traditions may place a little too much emphasis on angels, but there is certainly precedent for all thoughtful Christians to honor angels and even expect them to show up on God's command. In the Old Testament, God sent an army of angels with horses and chariots of fire to protect Elisha and his servant (2 Kings 6:8-23). Daniel describes how an angel shut the mouth of the lions he was facing (Daniel 6:22). In Acts 12, an angel helped Peter escape from prison. Paul faced a shipwreck with surprising calm because an angel had explained God's plan for the coming days (Acts 27:23-26).

It's also worth considering how often angels intervene and simply go undetected or unconfirmed. It's possible your own life has been spared a dozen times because your guardian angel cleared a path or guided you along a safer route.

So. Believe in angels. And tell your kids about angels. After all, angels are referred to more than 200 times in the Bible. [2]

Don't pray *to* your guardian angel, but certainly pray *for* God to send his angels to guide and protect those people who mean so much to you. Especially when you can't.

Prayer for God's Messengers and Protectors

Heavenly Father. I look forward someday to crossing over from this world into your heavenly realm. In the meantime, thank you for sending angels across that great divide. We count on your intervention in our lives, and it's pretty amazing that you might choose to send angels to guide us, guard us, and even rescue us from dangers in this fallen world. Thank you for angels! Praying in the name of your Son, Jesus. Amen.

∞

Do not forget to show hospitality to strangers, for by so doing some people have shown hospitality to angels without knowing it.

Hebrews 13:2

14

Pray Unexpectedly, Inescapably, and Irresistibly

Here's an idea I stole from another dad and have mentioned in two previous books. But it's so awesome and so on target that I had to include it here as well. I call this strategy "knock and pray."

It works for any kid at any age. It's something you can do today without any preparation. And it may launch them (and you) into a whole new intimacy in your prayer life with God and your relationship to each other.

They won't expect it. They can't escape it. And once you get going, they can't resist it. Ready?

Anytime day or night, knock on your son or daughter's bedroom door and say something like, "I need a quiet place to pray. Can I jump in here for about two minutes?" They may look up and blink a couple times, but I am pretty sure their response will be, "Umm. I guess so."

Then do it. Walk in, sit down on the edge of their bed, and almost as if they're not there start praying right out loud, but in a low tone of voice. Pray for your situation at work, your wife, your other kids, your own stresses, a neighbor, your community, and any other concerns you might have. End with a prayer for your own child who is sitting right there with you. Thank them, kiss their forehead, and leave quietly and gracefully.

Does that sound impossible? It's really not. It may be a bit out of your comfort zone, but that's part of the idea. You just need to be real.

Now make sure to keep it simple. And don't go too long. Two minutes or less. And then you're gone. Your child may be stunned by the experience. Or maybe it will make perfect sense to them. If they're four, they will love it and maybe think it's fun. If they're teenagers, they'll mull over it for a few minutes and then text their friends, "My dad did something totally weird. But kinda cool."

In any case, that two minutes you spent in your child's bedroom achieves about a dozen worthy goals. You prayed. You modeled how to pray. You let them know that you believe prayer works. You entered their world. You allowed them to enter your world. You let them know your marriage is strong. You reminded them that other members of the family have concerns that are equal to or greater than theirs. You let them know your schedule. And maybe your prayers helped unleash supernatural forces—such as legions of guardian angels—within the walls of that bedroom.

Perhaps best of all, you have earned the right to return in the near future to knock and pray again. My friend who first described this prayer strategy and gave me permission to share it related that, at first, his unannounced prayer visits were a bit of an intrusion upon his daughter's adolescent world. But he told her it was his responsibility as a father and she'd have to get used to it. Over the months and years, he began to pray for her heart, health, friends, future, and even her future husband, whoever that might be. At first, she just listened. Then she began to add her own prayers. Sometimes the prayer time led to an extended conversation about significant issues, conversations that might otherwise have never taken place.

So, knock gently and pray with warmth, sincerity, and sincere expectations. And don't be surprised if your kids start looking forward to your spontaneous prayers and even add some of their own.

Prayer for Two Minutes in Their World

Heavenly Father, thank you for the generosity and love you keep pouring on our family. I'm humbled and grateful. I'm challenged to serve you as best I can. You know how the media management project at work is stressing me out, and I need to ask you for some patience and some new direction. If you could guide my work this week, that would be great. For my family, you know Tim is waiting to hear back about those college applications. Help him trust you and make the right choice for next fall. And for Tammy, help me be the husband she needs. What a gift she is to me and our kids. Please, God, continue to bless our marriage. For Mr. Bradley's surgery. For safe travels next week as I head to Pittsburgh. For the election next month. Lord, please let your will be done in all these areas. Finally, for Megan. You've given her such a tender heart for others and a great sense of humor. Thank you. Help her to turn to you for all her decisions. Protect her always. I pray this is the name of your Son, Jesus. Amen.

❦

"Truly I tell you that if two of you on earth agree about anything they ask for, it will be done for them by my Father in heaven."

Jesus, in Matthew 18:19

15

Pray for a Faraway Friend

Five-year-old Rae Anne suddenly had a best friend. The charming and smiley red-haired girl from down the block was the perfect match for my feisty daughter. Neither was prissy or whiny or gossipy. They both had a competitive edge and weren't afraid to get dirty.

To celebrate their newfound friendship, I had a brilliant idea. A brilliant idea that backfired. That first summer I had Rae Anne and Hannah stand back-to-back on a stump in our backyard. I promised them we would take the same photo in the same place every year until they graduated high school. I confidently said that photo album would be a wonderful tribute to their lifelong friendship. They giggled at the thought of looking so far into the future. And they loved the idea.

That fall the little red-haired girl moved away. A thousand miles away.

Now if the two girls really had been friends for a decade or so, we might have had to make some bigger promises. To help Rae Anne get over the loss, we might have made promises of plane trips, coordinated vacation schedules, and all that.

But it turned out that Hannah was one of those summer friends that sweep in and out of your life. It's fun and wonderful. Then it's disappointing and painful. It's also pretty good practice for learning to let go of things and learning how so much of what we cherish here on earth is temporary. And it's a good chance to remind our kids that our home is in eternity.

But Rae Anne was five. And a little miffed. And of course there was daddy's photograph, which he had promised to replicate every summer. That photo was tangible evidence of a tear-filled loss.

Well, that unfortunate photograph turned out—for the most part— to be a blessing. After saying good-bye to Hannah, my daughter didn't know what to do with that photo that had been on her nightstand for really a short time, although it seemed like a lifetime to a five-year-old. Should she display it prominently or shove it in a drawer? Rita and I seized the moment. With that photograph as a prop, we reminded Rae Anne that Hannah was moving to a new place with no friends at all. And that the best thing a true friend could do would be to pray for a wonderful, fabulous, awesome *new* friend for Hannah.

Trooper that she is, Rae Anne joined us as we prayed. And even added some surprising and thoughtful prayers of her own for Hannah's mom, dad, and brother.

Was it hard? Sure. Did it make it easier for Rae Anne to let go of her best friend? Not really. But it was the right thing to do. As I recall, at last report Hannah was doing fine.

That entire episode from more than 15 years ago has made me appreciate all my children's friends even more.

The story shouldn't be told without this addendum. That photo remains in a small collection of Rae Anne's precious memories. Once in a while, just to torment me, Rae will bring it to my attention and thank me sarcastically for taking that heartwarming and historic series of photos (totaling one) with her best friend Hannah.

And that, in turn, reminds me that I should never, ever have introduced the art of sarcasm to my kids. For dads especially, it will always come back to haunt you.

Prayer for Friends Old and New

Heavenly Father. This is a prayer of gratitude. Thank you that you put people in our lives who know us and love us anyway. Family is awesome. And we're stuck with them and they're stuck with us. But friends are friends just because. Those relationships don't just happen by accident. We pray for friends old and new. We pray for friends we've lost and friends we'll meet in your timing. Help us be the kind of friends that can be counted on. Trusted. Faithful. Help us be friends who let some things slide but also have the courage to speak truth when our friends need to be held accountable. For Hannah, Joseph, Brayden, Riley, Natalie, and all the boys and girls who come in and out of our children's lives, please draw them close to you. Just like we need you, they do too! We love and trust you. In Jesus' name. Amen.

∞

One who has unreliable friends soon comes to ruin,
but there is a friend who sticks closer than a brother.

Proverbs 18:24

16

Pray Lullabies That May
Not Be Lullabies

If you're not a big fan of "Rock-a-Bye Baby" or don't see yourself as someone who can carry a tune, stick with me anyway.

As you've noticed, the 52 chapters in this book end with 52 *spoken* prayers. I believe God wants us to speak audible words when we pray. Romans 10:9 even includes spoken words as part of the instruction to gain eternal life: "If you declare with your mouth, 'Jesus is Lord,' and believe in your heart that God raised him from the dead, you will be saved." So let's keep speaking prayers right out loud.

I equally endorse silent prayer. But I didn't include any silent prayers in the book mostly because silent prayers are between you and God. Besides, a book filled with silent prayers would be mostly blank pages, right?

But singing as prayer (and prayer as singing) has a long-standing tradition in corporate worship, with kids at church camp, and with moms rocking babies to sleep.

The fourth-century theologian and philosopher Augustine is credited with the saying, "He who sings, prays twice." I'm not sure about the theology, but that's an uplifting magnet I'd put on my fridge. I could even point to it when my kids beg me to stop singing in the kitchen.

One of the great benefits of singing is that the words stick. In his eternal wisdom, God remembers every word of every prayer. Not so much with humans. Just a day or two after any spoken prayer, the limits of our brain capacity prevent us from retaining more than a phrase or two.

But for better or worse, we do remember song lyrics. And I can prove it. With apologies, I challenge you *not* to think of the words to "Itsy-Bitsy Spider" or the theme from *Gilligan's Island* or "Yellow Submarine."

The good news is that you probably also remember the words to "Amazing Grace," "Jesus Loves Me," and one or two lullabies your mom sang when you were just a moppet. Brain experts tell us that music makes up some of our earliest memories. Spend a moment pulling out those memories and hopefully your mind can move on from nursery rhymes, TV themes, and old rock 'n' roll lyrics.

Another great benefit of singing hymns and lullabies is that you already know these prayers. You may know a few memorized spoken prayers that you can access at any time. But the number of well-loved worship songs you know is practically endless. Consider: "Kumbaya," "Michael, Row the Boat Ashore," "I Come to the Garden Alone," "Softly and Tenderly," "How Great Thou Art," "The Old Rugged Cross," "Turn Your Eyes upon Jesus," "Rock of Ages," "God Is So Good," "He's Got the Whole World in His Hands," "How Great Is Our God," "His Banner over Me Is Love," "Just As I Am," and "Swing Low, Sweet Chariot."

Whatever your musical tastes, did you know you can sing any of your favorite songs in lullaby fashion? Just slow it down and sing in a gentle whisper. I know one dad who rocked his babies to sleep by softly and reverently singing Rich Mullins's "Awesome God" and DC Talk's "Jesus Freak." He remembers, "Those were my go-to lullabies. It knocked 'em out every time."

The next prayer time you're feeling songful or silly or empowered, try singing your prayers with your kids. It even works when you're a little too tuckered out yourself when you're tucking them in. Rest in the Lord in song, and they will too.

Prayer for Hearts Filled with Song

Heavenly Father. "*Swing low, sweet chariot, comin' for to carry me home. Swing low, sweet chariot, comin' for to carry me home. I looked over Jordan, and what did I see comin' for to carry me home? A band of angels comin' after me, comin' for to carry me home. Swing low, sweet chariot, comin' for to carry me home Swing low, sweet chariot, comin' for to carry me home. If you get there before I do...comin' for to carry me home...tell all my friends I'm comin' too. Comin' for to carry me home.*" *In Jesus' name. Amen.*

He put a new song in my mouth,
a hymn of praise to our God.
Many will see and fear the Lord
and put their trust in him.

Psalm 40:3

17

Pray Like This
(Matthew 6:9-13)

At least one of the Bibles in your house should be a red-letter edition. In those special editions, the publisher actually prints the words spoken by Jesus in red ink.

While every word of Scripture is "God-breathed and is useful for teaching, rebuking, correcting and training in righteousness" (2 Timothy 3:16), the words printed in red ink seem to take the privilege and immediate benefits of reading the Bible one step further. We imagine Jesus, the Son of God, walking right here on the same dusty earth on which we trudge and actually speaking those highlighted words.

Quite often he gives direct commands. "Come, follow me" (Mark 1:17), "Honor your father and mother" (Matthew 15:4), "Take and eat; this is my body" (Matthew 26:26). We like that. When it comes to God's Son, we appreciate being told very specifically what to do. It takes out the guesswork.

As you read this book on how, why, and when to pray for your kids, you'll be glad to know that Jesus instructed quite clearly, "This then, is how you should pray" (Matthew 6:9).

What comes next is commonly referred to as the Lord's Prayer. In the New International Version, it's only 66 words,* but not surprisingly, it covers everything you really need to consider when praying to God. Biblical scholars could spend countless days considering the meaning of each phrase, but let's see what we can glean in just a page or so.

---

* With the addition of the final line found in some later manuscripts and included, most famously, in the King James Version.

- *Our Father in heaven.* The Creator of the universe wants a relationship with each of us. He's real. And he's living in a place of eternal glory. He sent Jesus. He sent the Holy Spirit. But God the Father never leaves heaven.

- *Hallowed be your name.* Even God's *name* is set apart. Holy. Just mentioning his name unleashes unstoppable power.

- *Your kingdom come, your will be done.* Those are true statements. God reigns. God's will triumphs. But they are also prayer requests. We are asking God to send his Son back for his triumphant return. Soon. And we are surrendering our will for his. He knows what's best for us anyway.

- *On earth as it is in heaven.* These are two different places. But God is in control of both. Humans can't even begin to understand how the world and universe work. There's no way we can grasp the awesomeness of heaven.

- *Give us today our daily bread.* This is pretty straightforward. Except it's not just bread. And it's not just daily. God supplies all our needs. From oxygen to sunlight to the way our brain turns squiggly lines printed on the pages of this book into ideas on how to pray with our kids. How it all works together is God's gift to us.

- *Forgive us our debts, as we also have forgiven our debtors.* This could be considered the centerpiece of the gospel. We must acknowledge our brokenness and ask for God's forgiveness. It's the blood of Christ that washes away our sins. If we understand the critical nature and power of forgiveness, then we will also follow God's example. But our job is easier. All we have to do is forgive those who have wronged us, one person at a time. We can't begin to compare that to God's promise to forgive all the sins of all the people throughout history who believe and trust in him.

- *And lead us not into temptation, but deliver us from the evil one.* To be clear, God would never lead us into temptation.

But he did give us free will, which means he *allows* us to be tempted. Which means we need to ask him to save us from ourselves. The second part pinpoints the urgency. Satan is real. And we can't face him alone.

- *For yours is the kingdom and the power and the glory forever.* We've come full circle now. He's our Father in heaven. And his glory will last forever. He is the Alpha and the Omega.

- *Amen.* Amen.

If you grew up in a home that rattled off the Lord's Prayer in 11 seconds or less, try slowing it down. Especially with your kids. There's so much to be considered.

If the Lord's Prayer is not part of your regular prayer arsenal, you're missing out. Next time you have an occasion to pray with your kids, surprise them by not speaking your words, but the words of Jesus.

Prayer As Instructed

Heavenly Father. Your name is holy. Help us build your kingdom on earth, even as we wait for your Son to come in glory. Help us to seek, not our own will, but your will. Thank you that we can trust you for our needs. We know our sin separates us from you and breaks your heart. Forgive us, Lord. Thank you for sending Jesus to pay the price for those sins. Help us to be a healing force in your world. Protect us from the devil and his demons. We pray as Jesus prayed. Amen.

God so loved the world that he gave his one and only Son, that whoever believes in him shall not perish but have eternal life.

Jesus, in John 3:16

18

Pray for Their Rotten,
Terrible, Creepy Siblings

Not long ago we apologized to my adult son Alec.

Rita and I had spent most of the 1990s praying he would stop picking on his innocent little brother Max. Way too often we felt obliged to wield the hammer of parental authority on Alec with accusations, lectures, time-outs, and what we thought were appropriate punishments. It was truly stunning how often—for no apparent reason—Alec would start pounding on sweet, angelic Max. Alec, of course, claimed Max *deserved* to be pounded. But how was that possible?

Recently, watching an old home video, we figured it out. The video is a classic shot of our youngest, Rae Anne, gleefully tearing into her first birthday cake. All the attention in the room is on the little birthday girl. But just off to the side—almost unnoticeable—the camera captures seven-year-old Max reaching over and flicking the ear of thirteen-year-old Alec. In response, Alec turns and gives his little brother a well-deserved major shove. Suddenly the most perplexing Payleitner mystery of the '90s was solved.

Maximilian was not the victim, he was the provocateur. Alec was merely defending himself. Even worse, after years of getting away with close to murder, Max was getting bolder and bolder and sneakier and sneakier. The revealing video also captured the typical adult response to the common Alec–Max interaction. But it wasn't from Rita or me.

That day, my dad didn't see the initial tweak from his younger grandson, but he certainly saw the shove from his older grandson. Papa responded, "Alec! Be nice. Be nice to your brother." Yikes, even Papa was getting it wrong.

The good news is that by the time Alec went off to college, the two boys had matured to a level of mutual respect. The better news is that justice was ultimately served. After viewing that old video, Rita and I didn't hesitate to apologize to Alec for years of misjudging and mishandling our parental responsibilities in that specific scenario. Thankfully, he forgave us.

Later, when the entire family gathered to watch the video evidence of his long-ago wrongdoing, Max readily confessed but also insisted that he be credited for taking the art of persecuting older siblings to a new level. I must say, his technique was flawless. And the video was hilarious.

The lessons? There are several. First, go easy on doling out punishment to your kids for being kids. It may come back to bite you. Also, listen when your kids insist that what you thought you saw might not be exactly what happened. Finally, shoot plenty of videotape. It may come in handy later as evidence in the court of family justice.

What does all this have to do with prayer? Well, one year at a family camp, Rita picked up on a great strategy for dealing with sibling rivalry. When conflict flared up, she would put an immediate stop to it and "force" the dueling culprits to pray for each other and with each other. Right out loud. We didn't present it as a punishment. The goal was to pray God into the situation. Plus, it gave everyone involved a chance to consider how God has a unique viewpoint on every circumstance, how he is the ultimate judge, how forgiveness is powerful, and how family members should regularly be lifting each other up in prayer.

In their twenties and beyond, Alec and Max have grown wonderfully close. Maybe that's a direct answer to prayers they said for each other back when they were growing up and pounding each other.

Don't worry. Very little blood was actually shed.

Prayer for Siblings

Heavenly Father. Thanks for my kids. All of them. And when they start getting on each other's nerves, I still thank you for them. When the aggression starts or the decibel level rises, help me to respond in love. Help me to listen and discern and punish when necessary. I pray especially for Sydney and Caleb. Those two have been going at it too much for too long. Could you insert yourself right in the middle of their relationship? Help them find moments of appreciation for each other. Certainly, don't let their disagreements escalate into anything that becomes really hurtful or long-lasting. Thank you, Lord, for my family. We love and trust you. In Jesus' name. Amen.

Adam made love to his wife Eve, and she became pregnant and gave birth to Cain. She said, "With the help of the LORD I have brought forth a man." Later she gave birth to his brother Abel.

Genesis 4:1-2

19

Pray for Those
Who Persecute You

Know any contemptible jerks, creeps, or reprobates with seemingly no chance of redemption? I do.

I was thinking about including their first names or maybe just initials, but that might come back to bite me. So let's just say I'm thinking about three guys right now who I wouldn't miss if they fell off the face of the earth. I don't wish them harm. I would never do anything nasty to them. But if they could just go elsewhere so I would never have to deal with them again, that would upgrade my quality of life.

Does that make me a bad person? Maybe. But I'm not alone in these kinds of feelings. I know because you are also thinking of a person or two who falls in the same category. We all have enemies. Maybe your feelings aren't quite as shameful as mine, but you get a sense of what I'm talking about. It's natural to want to get even when we've been belittled, assaulted, ridiculed, mocked, scorned, bullied, robbed, or harassed. Our desire for revenge is even more natural if it's our children who are under attack.

Yes, it's natural. But it's also wrong. That's why we need a *supernatural* response. Under our own power, there's no way we can live up to the command, "Love your enemies and pray for those who persecute you."

Does that clear command from Matthew 5:44 still sound impossible? It is for nonbelievers. But those who trust God can count on the Holy Spirit to guide them. We can actually love our persecutors in the same way God loves them. We can pray for them, because we know God's intervention really can soften their hearts—and ours.

Beyond that, allow me to add a couple more biblical principles that may make this idea of loving your enemies even a little more manageable.

1. You can be sure they are not "getting away" with anything. Your enemies will have to settle up with God at a later date.

2. There is a way to utilize their malevolent nature to turn their life around. And since you are in direct contact with them, you just might be the right person for the job. The strategy described in Romans is this: kill 'em with kindness.

> *Do not repay anyone evil for evil. Be careful to do what is right in the eyes of everyone. If it is possible, as far as it depends on you, live at peace with everyone. Do not take revenge, my dear friends, but leave room for God's wrath, for it is written: "It is mine to avenge; I will repay," says the Lord. On the contrary: "If your enemy is hungry, feed him; if he is thirsty, give him something to drink. In doing this, you will heap burning coals on his head." Do not be overcome by evil, but overcome evil with good (Romans 12:17-21).*

What a brilliant concept. Treat your abrasive neighbors with dignity. Meet their needs, and your actions may shine light into darkness in their home for generations to come. Your sincere love, reluctant though it is, may open their eyes to how they've been acting. There's a good chance they rub everybody they meet the wrong way and don't have too many authentic friendships. Suddenly you come along and treat them with unconditional love and respect. Without a doubt, your display of grace will get their attention.

It may be hard to admit, but God loves your persecutors just as much as he loves you. It would be nice to be his favorite, but that's not the way it works. Besides, we are all far from perfect. We mess up all the time. That's the sinful nature of man.

Which takes us back to the Lord's Prayer, which asks God to "forgive us our debts, as we also have forgiven our debtors." In other words, if we really want to get right with God, we probably have to reduce our revenge-seeking and any long-standing animosity by about 100 percent.

This is one of those concepts our kids need to learn but that requires a teachable moment. You'll want to lay the groundwork and be patient for the right situation.

In the meantime, you can pray that your kids don't get scarred by the thoughtless words or attitudes of those who seem to think their life purpose is to make other miserable. That includes frustrated teachers, playground bullies, jealous classmates, ornery neighbors, judgmental aunts, and pigheaded coaches.

The good news is that you have been given the privilege of praying for them. Maybe your prayers—and a generous serving of hot coals on their head—will keep them from hurting anyone else.

Prayer for Those You Don't Want to Pray For

Heavenly Father. I know there are Christians around the world who are truly being persecuted for their faith. Enduring incarceration, beatings, arson, and murder. I pray for healing and protection for those brave believers. But as a parent, I can't stand the idea of my children being ridiculed or bullied. Please protect Allison and Anthony. And yes—I do pray for those who would hurt me or my children in that way. If you can give me the strength, Lord, I will even try to show kindness and mercy to these enemies. I pray this in the name of your Son, Jesus. Amen.

Live such good lives among the pagans that, though they accuse you of doing wrong, they may see your good deeds and glorify God on the day he visits us.

1 Peter 2:12

20

Pray Like Hannah

Have you ever been so desperate that you made an outlandish promise to God? It happens all the time with fictional characters on TV and the movies. And in real life too. A guy in a tavern promises to give up drinking if he wins the lottery. Desperate parents promise to go back to church if God brings back their runaway teenager.

Back during my freshman year of college, I may even have prayed something like, "Oh God, I know I fell asleep during most of my Introduction to Modern Philosophy classes, but if you'd just let me pass I'll be extra nice to doggies and kitties for the rest of my life." Yikes. Please forgive me for my self-centered prayer and embarrassing attempt to bargain with God. That occurred before I really understood how prayer worked. Although somehow I did get a B-minus in that course.

Anyway, back around 1100 BC, Hannah offered an even more outlandish prayer and promise to God. And it turned out to be part of a turning point in the history of the world. For those who don't know the story, Hannah lived during a time of transition for Israel. After being ruled by judges for many generations, the people are looking around at other nearby countries and thinking it was time they had a king.

Hannah happens to be one of two wives married to a man named Elkanah. The other wife, Peninnah, has several children, but the Bible tells us that Elkanah "loved Hannah, but the LORD had closed her womb" (1 Samuel 1:5 NASB). The next verses explain how Peninnah seems to take great pleasure in mocking and harassing Hannah year after year for her childless condition. Elkanah cares deeply for Hannah, but tears flow often. One desperate day near the Lord's temple, Hannah prays,

> *LORD Almighty, if you will only look on your servant's misery*
> *and remember me, and not forget your servant but give her*
> *a son, then I will give him to the LORD for all the days of his*
> *life, and no razor will ever be used on his head (1 Samuel 1:11).*

Sitting not far away, Eli the priest doesn't hear the prayer, but does see Hannah overflowing with emotion and apparently muttering to herself. Eli even chastises Hannah for being drunk. Respectfully, Hannah explains she had not been drinking, but was pouring out her heart to the Lord. Without even knowing what she had been praying for, the priest states with assurance, "Go in peace, and may the God of Israel grant you what you have asked of him" (1 Samuel 1:17). At that moment, the sadness lifts from Hannah and it isn't long before she gives birth to a son. She names the boy Samuel, which means, "Because I asked the LORD for him."

With her husband's blessing, Hannah keeps her promise and delivers young Samuel to serve under Eli. The next several chapters reveal God calling the boy into ministry and his expanding role as a respected prophet and Israel's final and most influential judge. Samuel even anoints the first two kings of Israel, Saul and David.

All of which entices us to take another look at Hannah's prayer. She was praying out of desperation, but she didn't overpromise. Indeed, she wanted a child. She was probably even envious of Peninnah and wanted to present Elkanah with an heir. When she kept her vow and left the boy with Eli at the tabernacle for a lifetime of service, it would be reasonable to assume she would be filled with grief. But that wasn't the case.

> *Then Hannah prayed and said:*
> *"My heart rejoices in the LORD;*
> *in the LORD my horn is lifted high.*
> *My mouth boasts over my enemies,*
> *for I delight in your deliverance.*
> *There is no one holy like the LORD;*
> *there is no one besides you;*
> *there is no Rock like our God."*
>
> *1 Samuel 2:1-2*

Hannah trusted God. She rejoiced in his ultimate control over her life. This prayer goes on for more than 20 lines without any hint of remorse or regret concerning the son she had just given up. She was still a mom and would still be part of his life, but Samuel now belonged 100 percent to God.

As parents, that's our goal, right? Bible scholars suggest that Samuel was three years old at the time. Most of us parents hang on to our children for quite a bit longer. But not even that is guaranteed.

Hannah's prayer of surrender was, "I will give him to the Lord for all the days of his life." Can you match that sacrificial prayer?

Prayer of All Parents

Heavenly Father. Help us never forget that our children are gifts from you. And our ultimate task is to prepare them for service and give them back to you, the life-giver. Hannah's story reminds us of so many things. How we should delight in you. How we should never take our children for granted. How so many women and men desperately want children. The preciousness of life. And how God can use a mom and a boy to do great things for his kingdom. Lord, we trust you with our lives. And it's hard, but we trust you also with the lives of our children we love so much. We pray in the name of your Son, Jesus. Amen.

The eyes of the Lord range throughout the earth to strengthen those whose hearts are fully committed to him.

2 Chronicles 16:9

21

Pray Big...and Trust God

When my daughter was 11 she mentioned one of her dreams to God. *Might there be a place for me on the U.S. Olympic softball team?* Rae Anne even targeted 2012 and 2016 as potential Olympic years. That was clearly one of those prayers that might take a decade to come true. And that's okay. God sees all time and space at this very moment. Praying can impact events in the next two minutes. And prayers can also be answered in half a lifetime. It's a great sign when your son or daughter has a long-term vision and asks God to help lay a foundation for future events.

When Rae Anne was 12, the International Olympic Committee announced they were dropping softball as an Olympic sport.

Sometimes prayers are answered sooner than you think. And sometimes that answer is no. It was crystal clear that Rae Anne would never represent her country on a softball diamond.

Well, she didn't give up on the game she loved. Her Olympic dream was no longer a topic of discussion, but she set a new goal of playing Division 1 softball. In high school, she set some school records and received some statewide recognition. By her junior year, she was ambitiously contacting coaches of universities with great academics and great softball programs.

After jumping through all kind of hoops and meeting all kinds of strict criteria, Rae Anne was accepted into the U.S. Military Academy at West Point. Pretty impressive.

Now maybe you already see where this story is headed. I didn't until Rita and I traveled to West Point and saw the Army softball team line up for the national anthem. There was my daughter standing at attention on the third-base line with 15 teammates. The music starts and every one of those young women snap a perfect salute and hold it through the last line of the song: "O say, does that star-spangled banner yet wave o'er the land of the free and the home of the brave?"

My daughter was almost miraculously playing on America's team. A softball team—part of the larger Army team—that worked harder in the course of a year than any other. The Black Knights of West Point.

It's a fact that no softball team from any country made it to London in 2012 or Rio in 2016. But in 2013 Rae Anne and her teammates stood on the third-base line saluting the flag and representing her country for the NCAA tournament at the University of Texas at Austin. Rita and I will never forget it, and neither will Rae.

It may sound like I'm bragging. And perhaps I am a little. But it's a true story. A story of the prayers of a young girl answered in an unexpected way. Hearing it might encourage your daughter or son to dream big and pray big. And to not get discouraged when things aren't working out exactly as you planned. There's a good chance that God has other plans and other ways to answer your prayers.

Prayer for God's Will

Heavenly Father. You know the desires of our hearts. You know our needs. But still we come to you with our requests, hopes, and dreams. Thank you for listening. Thank you for loving us. Thank you for sometimes giving us exactly what we ask for. And thanks also for sometimes not. Keep surprising us with glorious sunrises, kind words from strangers, giggles of small children, and generous gifts of which we are not worthy. Above all, help us trust you, and help us always remember that you hold us in the palm of your hand. We love you, and we do trust you. In Jesus' name. Amen.

"Ask and it will be given to you; seek and you will find; knock and the door will be opened to you. For everyone who asks receives; the one who seeks finds; and to the one who knocks, the door will be opened.

"Which of you, if your son asks for bread, will give him a stone? Or if he asks for a fish, will give him a snake? If you, then, though you are evil, know how to give good gifts to your children, how much more will your Father in heaven give good gifts to those who ask him!"

Jesus, in Matthew 7:7-11

22

Pray Through the Desert

In your prayer life, I trust that you've experienced seasons during which you felt connected, guided, loved, and embraced. God spoke, you listened, and it all worked out. You prayed for your kindergartner to wake up with dry sheets, and bed-wetting became a thing of the past. You prayed for a friend for your son starting middle school, and he comes home talking about the really cool guys with lockers on either side of his. You prayed for a more respectful teenager, and out of the blue she complimented your new haircut. Life for a season was…refreshing.

But now you're stuck in the middle of a spiritual desert—feeling lost and far from God. Let me suggest some steps you can take.

1. Acknowledge that God didn't move, you did. After all, he never changes. He is still eager to spend time with you. Ask yourself if his inspired Word is gathering dust on the other side of the room. Remind yourself that he loves you as much now as ever.

2. Consider whether you may have been fooled into experimenting with another power source. God is still the ultimate source of energy, but for some reason maybe you pulled the plug. If so, being lost in the desert is proof that no one else can match the staying power of the Creator of the universe.

3. Realize you're not alone. As a matter of fact, every emotion you're having was also experienced by Jesus. He knew his death on the cross was part of a heavenly plan, but still he felt abandoned. He even cried out, "My God, my God, why have you forsaken me?" (Matthew 27:46).

4. Trust that your condition is temporary. The Israelites wandered in the desert for 40 years, but eventually they reached the Promised Land. Your dry journey will surely last less than four decades.

5. Realize there is life in the desert. It may seem desolate, but a teeming community of reptiles, desert mammals, and other creatures live just beneath the surface of the sand. Cacti survive on very little moisture. You may find an oasis just over the next dune. Desert dweller John the Baptist fulfilled prophecy and delivered the most important news in the history of the world strolling from one dusty town to another. He was "a voice of one calling in the wilderness, 'Prepare the way for the Lord, make straight paths for him'" (Mark 1:3). And he did all that without sunglasses or sunscreen.

6. Ask God, "What's next?" You may be surprised. Your desert exile might be a season of quiet, preparing you for explosive growth and impact. Before he performed any recorded miracles, Jesus voluntarily spent 40 days fasting in the desert enduring Satan's well-documented temptations. The next three years changed everything.

So next time you or your kids think you're in a spiritual desert, think again. Maybe even try to enjoy the sun on your face and the sand between your toes. Because in the very near future you may be put back to work. As he did with John the Baptist, God may ask you to be a loud, clear voice announcing the coming of Christ right where you are.

Prayer for Living Water

Heavenly Father. We yearn to be close to you. We much prefer exciting mountaintop experiences to the apparent dry desolation of the desert. But we trust you to work all things for the good. We understand that surviving a season in the desert might be just what we need for the next season of new life. Thank you for giving me the Living Water of your Son, Jesus, so that I may never be thirsty and never be without purpose in life. Amen.

Even though I walk
through the darkest valley,
I will fear no evil,
for you are with me;
your rod and staff,
they comfort me.

Psalm 23:4

23

Pray That They Don't Get Put in a Box

By middle school—or earlier—most kids get stuck with a label such as *math nerd, jock, bookworm, class clown, musician, wallflower, natural leader, techie, genius, cheerio, dreamer, slacker, drama geek, loner, princess, flirt, overachiever,* or *underachiever*. And, that's dangerous territory. Even the positive-sounding labels put a limit on who they are and what they can achieve.

When a child gets a label—even if it's just based on a passing character trait or one-time experience—it can stick for a long time. Often the child starts to believe it. So do friends. And teachers. And parents. It can be a self-perpetuating stereotype. It's a box that's hard to escape.

Who puts them in that box? Well, Mom and Dad, sometimes it's you. Your words. Your expectations. Your attitude. Parents have a natural, healthy desire to help their kids find their niche, but we can also have a not-so-healthy tendency to live vicariously through them.

Sometimes it's birth order that sticks on a label that may not be accurate. Your oldest is the leader or perfectionist. Your middle child is the conformist or mediator. The baby is the charming free spirit who really never follows through on responsibilities.

Another way parents label kids is by giving them excuses when they fail or don't fit in. *"Don't feel bad if (blank) happened. After all you're a (blank) kind of person. All you have to do is be true to yourself."*

It's also possible a well-meaning teacher, coach, sibling, grandparent, or mentor may have seen a glimmer of promise in your son or daughter and guided them down a certain path that really isn't the best fit. Worse, a shortsighted cynic in authority may have looked at one bad choice your child happened to make and crammed them in a crate labeled "only good for one thing" or "zero potential."

Your kids may be comfy in their box, or not so much. But especially if he or she was labeled early, a wise parent will make sure their child knows they very likely have a variety of gifts not limited to a single box. Da Vinci was a well-respected artist, but he didn't rest on those accolades. He was also a mathematician, a mapmaker, a civil engineer, a botanist, and the inventor of musical instruments, hydraulic pumps, a steam cannon, and several flying machines. More recently, A.C. Gilbert invented the Erector Set only after working his way through Yale Medical School as a magician and winning an Olympic gold medal in the pole vault. Dr. William Moulton Marston was a Harvard-educated psychologist, but he also invented the modern lie detector and created Wonder Woman.

Those are great stories to tell your children to help open their hearts and minds to different ways God can use them. In your own neighborhood, you might very well find an English teacher who makes cabinets, a marketing manager who collects butterflies, or a football coach who plays bass guitar at church on Sundays.

The Bible says, "In his grace, God has given us different gifts for doing certain things well" (Romans 12:6 NLT). I haven't found any Scripture that limits individuals to a single talent or ability. But the Bible does often emphasize the idea of discovering and using your talents to give glory to God. And that there is "a time for everything, and a season for every activity under the heavens" (Ecclesiastes 3:1).

One word of caution. When you pray with your child about their future, it's natural to connect their current hobbies and activities with a college major or career path. That's also dangerous territory. Praying is talking to God. If you want to talk with your kids about exploring their gifts and maybe kick around new areas of interests or how to further sharpen a skill, that's awesome. But hold that conversation before or after prayer, not during.

Don't let your prayers become career counseling sessions. But do pray that your child has a chance to discover and enjoy all their God-given gifts.

Prayer for How to Use Gifts

Heavenly Father. Thank you for the many gifts you have given to Abigail. Thank you for the ones that are so evident. Her sense of humor. Her love of books. Her competitive spirit. The way she really thinks things through. Thank you also for the gifts she has that haven't shown up yet. You have a future in store for Abby we can't even imagine. Help her to serve you with all her gifts. In career choices. In her hobbies. In ministry. Help me come alongside her at the right time and be an encourager and partner. Amen.

Each of you should use whatever gift you have received to serve others, as faithful stewards of God's grace in its various forms.

1 Peter 4:10

24

Pray with Both Persistence
and Consistency

The question resonated with just about everyone in the room. During weekly gatherings, our summer small group of about a dozen regulars experienced much uplifting conversation and debate. But this question left us feeling a bit guilty and a little disappointed in ourselves. The gist of the question was, "When I set aside a block of time to really pray, why do I allow myself to be distracted? Why do I frequently start thinking about my list of things that need doing and let my mind wander down all kinds of rabbit trails that take me away from communication with God?"

You can relate to that question, right? We imagine medieval monks living in silent prayer year after year. We hear about a pastor on the other side of the world imprisoned for leading an underground church praying with intensity and focus for months before his release. We accept the fact we're not spiritual giants, but we really would like to pray ten minutes straight without being interrupted by our own random thoughts. Often distractions come one after another. In the middle of our intentional prayer time, we make a mental note to pick up a gallon of milk. Something triggers a thought about the new noise coming out of our dishwasher. Then we get distracted wondering why we so often get distracted. By the end of our prayer time, we feel totally inferior to the woman down the street who sets aside an hour every day to pray for her grandkids.

Thankfully, one of the regular members of the group was our warm and wonderful pastor. He gave us all a perspective worth sharing. And worth remembering when we're interacting with our children about the topic of prayer.

"Don't judge prayer," he recommended. "God is delighted anytime an individual makes a choice to come before him in prayer. Someone who can stay focused on prayer for an hour at a time chooses to pray only *once*. But the person who gets distracted during prayer might choose *more than a dozen* times in an hour to come before God. You can be sure he loves the persistent pray-er just as much as he loves the consistent pray-er."

Luke chapter 18 opens with two parables that address the issue of effective prayer. The first confirms that God moves when we persevere in bringing our requests before him. This passage is often called "The Parable of the Persistent Widow."

> One day Jesus told his disciples a story to show that they should always pray and never give up. "There was a judge in a certain city," he said, "who neither feared God nor cared about people. A widow of that city came to him repeatedly, saying, 'Give me justice in this dispute with my enemy.' The judge ignored her for a while, but finally he said to himself, 'I don't fear God or care about people, but this woman is driving me crazy. I'm going to see that she gets justice, because she is wearing me out with her constant requests!'" (Luke 18:1-5 NLT).

The second parable is an excellent reminder for anyone who thinks they deserve a gold medal for their ability to pray better, longer, or stronger than the guy in the next pew. Prayer is not a competition. It's how we humbly surrender to God's will for our lives.

> To some who were confident of their own righteousness and looked down on everyone else, Jesus told this parable: "Two men went up to the temple to pray, one a Pharisee and the other a tax collector. The Pharisee stood by himself and prayed: 'God, I thank you that I am not like other people—robbers, evildoers, adulterers—or even like this tax collector. I fast twice a week and give a tenth of all I get.'
>
> "But the tax collector stood at a distance. He would not even look up to heaven, but beat his breast and said, 'God, have mercy on me, a sinner.'

"I tell you that this man, rather than the other, went home justified before God. For all those who exalt themselves will be humbled, and those who humble themselves will be exalted" (Luke 18:9-14).

Moms and dads, let's pledge to carve out significant chunks of time on a regular basis to pray long and hard for our kids. Let's also pledge to pray during and between the distractions of life with frequent short bursts of prayer on their behalf.

Finally, let's not compare how we pray with how others pray except to remember that coming before God in humility and brokenness wins out every time over the guy who crows, "Hear ye! Hear ye! All take notice of my awesome ability to pray and how awesome I am in my awesomeness!"

Prayer About Prayer

Heavenly Father. I come before you with a focused mind and heart desiring to serve you in all things with all my life. Still, I confess to being distracted by the events and expectations of living in this fallen world. Thank you for carrying me through those times when I forget momentarily that every breath and every good gift comes from you. Help me be a persistent and humble prayer warrior. And help me be a model for my children in coming to you consistently and persistently in all things. I pray in the name of your Son, Jesus. Amen.

⌒⌒

Devote yourselves to prayer, being watchful and thankful.

Colossians 4:2

25

Pray A-C-T-S

Hang around enough Sunday-school lessons and you'll hear all kinds of mnemonic devices for remembering books of the Bible and other facts.

To remember the five books of Moses, you could teach your kids "God's Excellent Love Never Dies." A statement which, of course, is true. And it also happens to correspond with the initials of the Torah (a.k.a. Pentateuch). But it's probably easier and more effective to simply have your kids remember "Genesis Exodus Leviticus Numbers Deuteronomy."

Similarly, instead of teaching them to "Go Eat PopCorn," why not just have them remember "Galatians Ephesians Philippians Colossians"?

One of my favorite memory-jogging tricks was using the word *baptism* to remember the names of the apostles. Replace the "i" with "j" and you have the first name initials for all 12 apostles named in Matthew 10:2-4: Bartholomew, Andrew, Peter, Philip, Thomas, Thaddeus, James the son of Zebedee, James the son of Alphaeus, John, Judas, Simon the Cananaean, and Matthew the tax collector.

But when it comes to prayer, I'm not sure you can get any more down to the core of why and how to pray than with the four letters *A-C-T-S. Adoration. Confession. Thanksgiving. Supplication.* Perhaps those are old-sounding words. They are certainly long ones—between nine and twelve letters. But A-C-T-S is a classic method, well worth passing on, for triggering and encouraging prayer. If your kids hang around the church long enough, they'll hear it from some Sunday-school teacher or youth volunteer. So they might as well hear it from you. They may even try to give you credit for inventing it, but don't let them. You'll just have to find satisfaction in being the first to introduce them to the idea.

The word *Adoration* triggers the idea of being so blown away by the awesomeness and power of God that I am forced to my knees. He is worthy to be praised. He's not just more magnificent than the Grand Canyon or Mount Everest—he is the Creator of those natural wonders. If we start our prayers with humble adoration of a glorious God, we're headed in the right direction.

Confession gets the crud out of the way so we can pray from a clean slate. And I get that. I know it's hard for my wife to enjoy her morning coffee if the kitchen is dirty. God already knows my sins and shortcomings, but I need to do my own personal inventory as part of the cleanup. He also knows whether I have an attitude of repentance. The act of confessing our sins to him begins the process of breaking the pattern of sin in our lives. Confession is surely designed more for us than for him. When we come to God for forgiveness, he has already forgotten our sins, casting them away as far "as the east is from the west" (Psalm 103:12).

After we acknowledge God's grandeur and come clean before him, *Thanksgiving* reminds us that it's time to say "thanks." Thanks for life. Thanks for supplying all our needs. Thanks for the good stuff and the bad, because he uses it all to make us more like him.

Only then can we even think about *Supplication* and asking God to "supply" this or that. It's actually kind of amusing to think our puny minds have any idea of what we really need. The best prayer to God is "Your will be done." But because he loves us and has given us free will, he wants to know the desires of our hearts.

So teach your kids to pray *Adoration, Confession, Thanksgiving,* and *Supplication.* In that order. And I think those four ideas cover just about every prayer you can imagine.

Prayer All Ways

Heavenly Father. You are worthy of adoration. We confess to you those times when we have chosen to not follow you. We thank you for loving us even when we are not worthy of your love. And please continue to meet all our needs. We trust you in all things. Help us draw near to you and not take prayer for granted. We pray in the name of your Son, Jesus. Amen.

Do not be anxious about anything, but in everything, by prayer and petition, with thanksgiving, present your requests to God.

Philippians 4:6

26

Pray for Spiritual Protection

Today, my five kids are out of the house and my mortgage is almost paid off. I don't do it often, but if I impulsively spend $130 on something that's not really a necessity, I don't feel guilty about it. But flash back about 20 years and you're talking a whole different story. I had a new job, my family schedule was entering warp speed, and every nickel counted.

That's why, initially, Rita thought I had been a little frivolous when I came home from our local Christian bookstore with a piece of framed art that cost more than we could afford. But when she saw the lithograph *Spiritual Warfare* by Ron DiCianni and realized the depth of my feelings for what the image represented, she understood. That was about the time I left Michigan Avenue advertising to take a job producing Christian radio.

There were a lot of changes and uncertainties in the Payleitner family. Most of it was centered on our learning curve surrounding the Bible, harvesting our spiritual gifts, and how best to respond to God's call in our lives. Rita and I had recently done a life-changing spiritual pilgrimage overseas. We were about to change churches, which probably wasn't going to sit well with either set of parents. Plus, I was no longer writing ads and commercials for Midway Airlines, canned vegetables, and Corona Beer. My new career path was allowing me to use my creative gifts and experience to spread the message of the Josh McDowell Ministry, the Bible League, and the Salvation Army.

There's a very real chance that Satan was not happy about most of that.

When I saw the image of the man fervently praying over his sleeping son and angels doing battle outside the bedroom window, I knew it reflected my life, especially at that time. We hung the artwork outside my oldest son's bedroom.

If you don't know the painting, you may want to take a peek online. Search for "Spiritual Warfare by Ron DiCianni." Ron was the artist who illustrated the cover for the hugely popular novel on spiritual warfare, *This Present Darkness* by Frank Peretti. Ron's description of the painting I had purchased says much about the need to pray protection over our kids.

> Most people think that the centerpiece of the painting is the angels fighting in the window. It's not. The focus of the painting is the shadow of the cross that's falling on the father and son. Without that, as the assurance of our protection, I would be too afraid to approach the subject! I used some symbolism in parts of the painting that sometimes get overlooked at first glance. Look at the father's watch—it is almost striking midnight. It was my way of saying that the "hour" (of time) is late, but also that if a dad is still up at that time praying for his child after a long day of work, I believe that God will honor that perseverance. Look also at the drapes blowing gently from open windows. I wanted to make the point that mere glass or wood could not prevent evil forces from getting to us but that prayer will! Another point of false hope is the wallpaper border of "Noah's Ark" that adorns the room. Certainly I am in favor of wall hangings and positive messages, but not as an end in themselves.
>
> Accessorizing our rooms will do very little if we don't pray. Our enemy knows that and would be content with all the "stuff" in the world hanging there. What Satan doesn't want is the prayer of a righteous man over his family. [3]

That piece of inspired artwork by a mere human painter served as a regular reminder to pray for each of my kids. Not just that they would stay healthy, get good grades, or win their next baseball game. I prayed for protection from spiritual attack—even those battles parents may never even know about. It wasn't until later that I realized how many of my children's friends and other members of our community were being targeted by Satan and his dark forces. I credit prayer for protecting my family from the worst of what the adversary had in mind.

Even now, writing this, I think back two decades ago and realize that my prayers have softened. The spiritual battle most certainly continues on. But today, without the kids underfoot, I'm not actively doing my part. My recent prayers have been probably more for provision than protection. With this keystroke, I pledge that the battle begins anew. Will you join me on behalf of your own family?

Prayer for the Spiritual Battle

Heavenly Father. I believe that the ultimate victory has already been won. But until Satan's final fall, we are in a battle for the hearts and minds of our children, our children's children, and our friends and neighbors. I trust that prayer unleashes, equips, and strengthens your angels. We implore you to draw us to our knees on behalf of those angels fighting the good fight in your name. We pray in the name of your Son, Jesus, who won the greatest battle on the cross and rising from the tomb. Amen.

◦◦◦

Our struggle is not against flesh and blood, but against the rulers, against the authorities, against the powers of this dark world and against the spiritual forces of evil in the heavenly realms.

Ephesians 6:12

27

Pray They Stick with It

In my opinion, the best half hour of scripted television ever produced was an episode from the second season of *The Wonder Years* titled "Coda." The critically acclaimed show highlighted the life and voiceover memories of a suburban middle-school boy, Kevin Arnold, growing up in the late '60s and early '70s. (Full disclosure: that's exactly when I was in middle school.)

The show aired from 1988 to 1993, and I assume that most parents raising kids today saw at least a few episodes when it first aired or in reruns. If I sat down to watch this episode, it would still put a lump in my throat and a tear in my eye. With your permission, let me walk you through the uncomplicated plotline.

As in every episode, the voice of Kevin as an adult establishes the theme. We see the boy Kevin stopping on his bike in front of a home down the block. For a moment, he thoughtfully watches a gathering through the curtains of the front picture window. A boy is playing the piano: Pachelbel's Canon in D Major. As we watch Kevin, the voiceover reveals just a hint of regret.

> *Narrator*: When you're a little kid you're a little bit of everything. Artist, scientist, athlete, scholar. Sometimes it seems like growing up is the process of giving those things up one by one. I guess we all have one thing we regret giving up. One thing we really miss. That we gave up because we were too lazy. Or we couldn't stick it out. Or because we were afraid.

The screenplay by Todd W. Langen beautifully captures the angst of a middle-school boy who may have some hidden talent for music, as he weighs all his options. Should he practice his scales or play football in the street with his pals? The decision to stick it out and really invest your heart is not easy. Much easier is the decision to quit, because then your worries are over. Exploring untapped talents is a risk. Every middle-schooler has a fear of failure or looking stupid.

The climactic scene occurs the night before the recital in the piano teacher's front parlor. At this dress rehearsal, Kevin watches in horror as the brown-nosing Ronald Hirschmuller robotically plays the Canon in D Major without missing a note but also without any emotion. Kevin's middle-school mind doesn't realize his nemesis's performance was staccato and lifeless. When Kevin sits down to perform the same piece—which he had practiced and mastered at home—he chokes. So to avoid embarrassment, he skips the recital. And he never plays piano again. And his talent goes untapped. Before the credits roll, we return to the scene that opened the episode. Straddling his bike, Kevin watches Ronald Hirschmuller play the piece and the final voice-over breaks your heart.

> *Narrator*: I remember the darkness falling at I sat there on the street looking in. And now, more than twenty years later, I still remember every note of the music that wandered out into the still night air. The only thing is, I can't remember how to play it anymore.

To this day, I can't hear Pachelbel's Canon in D Major without thinking of Kevin Arnold and all the other millions of young teenagers who gave up on something worthwhile. Music, dance, sports, theater, painting, sculpting, poetry, model rocketry, magic, martial arts, filmmaking, figure skating, AWANA, Boy Scouts, Girl Scouts—any activity in which it pays to start young and stick with it.

Sure, no kid can do it all. And many kids do too much. Plus, as the voice-over said in the opening monologue, "Growing up is a process of giving up those things one by one." But wouldn't it be great if our kids could all find one or two passions early, which would allow them to really invest the time and effort to become highly skilled? The idea is to choose a pursuit that might lead to career and even ministry opportunities.

Perseverance is a common theme throughout Scripture. But most of the time the concept refers to finishing the spiritual race, continually seeking God's will, and praying with tenacity.

> *I have fought the good fight, I have finished the race, I have kept the faith (2 Timothy 4:7).*
>
> *You need to persevere so that when you have done the will of God, you will receive what he has promised (Hebrews 10:36).*
>
> *Pray in the Spirit on all occasions with all kinds of prayers and requests. With this in mind, be alert and always keep on praying for all the Lord's people (Ephesians 6:18).*

The question might be, "Is there a connection between sticking with earthly pursuits (like piano lessons) and pursuing God's plan for your life?"

I think so. Of course, our children are not TV characters on a TV sitcom. But that's good news. It means we have more than 22 minutes of airtime to help them identify and nurture their gifts. Some gifts they're born with. Some are spiritual gifts received when Christ enters their lives. Some gifts they might discover early, set aside, and come back to with great diligence later in life.

Our children will be well served far into their adult years if we help them identify and nurture their spiritual leanings at an early age. Proverbs says, "Train up a child in the way he should go, even when he is old he will not depart from it" (Proverbs 22:6 NASB).

There are all kinds of ways to discover our children's inclinations. We can open new doors, administer assessment tests, introduce them to mentors, provide them with tools, sign them up for introductory classes, and quiz their teachers about how our kids compare to other kids. At the very least, we should spend enough time with our children to know their passions and preferences. That all may sound like overkill, but it's really not. As a parent, this is all part of your job description.

But even if they do find a pursuit that exactly fits their personality and giftedness, they still need to stick with it. Mom and Dad, to break through into that part of their mind and heart that controls perseverance, don't heap on guilt, wield strict parental authority, or provoke dreams of worldly fame and fortune. You want their passion for a pursuit to come from God. And prayer is the conduit.

I am pretty sure that Kevin's mom and dad didn't pray for his piano-playing passions. But if Mr. or Mrs. Arnold—or Kevin himself—would have prayed for piano perseverance during that pivotal weekend in his life, the voice-over at the end would have been singing a different tune.

Prayer for Passionate Pursuits

Heavenly Father. As Creator, you made us in your image. Which means you made us to be creative—using the arts and sciences to give you glory. Help us as parents to enter our children's lives so that we recognize their talents and gifts. But more than that, please open Emily's and Daniel's hearts to lifelong passions that bring them a rich and satisfying life. And give them exciting avenues to pursue while reminding them always to sincerely and humbly give the glory back to you. We pray in the name of your Son, Jesus. Amen.

He put a new song in my mouth,
a hymn of praise to our God.
Many will see and fear the LORD
and put their trust in him.

Psalm 40:3

28

Pray Away Demons

Pray away demons? You're thinking:

Really, Jay? I've misplaced two credit cards, my cellphone is cracked, I left a gallon of milk in the car overnight, the dog has tapeworms, my daughter has another new ear piercing, the toilet in the guest room has been running for two weeks, and you want me to worry about demons? *Something I can't see and am not sure exists?*

Well, yes. I can't help you with your spoiled milk, sick doggy, or cracked cellphone. But demons are something you need to be aware of. I'm not talking about pretend movie monsters, ghosts, or boogeymen. I'm referring to fallen angels who joined Satan in rebellion against God.

They most certainly exist. In his three years of public ministry, Jesus drove out demons from a variety of people, including two men who lived in a graveyard (Matthew 8:8), a man who could not talk (Matthew 9:33), another man who was blind and mute (Matthew 12:22), the young daughter of a Greek woman (Mark 7:26), and a man in a Capernaum synagogue (Luke 4:33). The last chapter of Mark reveals that Jesus had even driven seven demons out from Mary Magdalene. Perhaps gratitude for freedom from Satan's influence was the reason she was so passionate about following and serving Jesus.

Today, verifying the authenticity of specific claims of demon possession is difficult. Some addictions, cult activities, witchcraft, abnormal fears, and mental illness might possibly be the result of demonic activity. That doesn't absolve the victim of any responsibility. In most cases, those individuals cracked the door or took a voluntary step that led to a down-spiraling and slippery slope. Whether demons are involved or not, rescue from some of these desperate scenarios is virtually impossible unless the person turns to Jesus Christ.

An occasionally unruly teenager is probably not possessed by a demon. But it's possible. An examination of Matthew 17:14-20 may shed light on how one father came before Jesus to heal his demon-possessed son.

> When [Jesus, Peter, James, and John] came to the crowd, a man approached Jesus and knelt before him. "Lord, have mercy on my son," he said. "He has seizures and is suffering greatly. He often falls into the fire or into the water. I brought him to your disciples, but they could not heal him."
>
> "You unbelieving and perverse generation," Jesus replied, "how long shall I stay with you? How long shall I put up with you? Bring the boy here to me." Jesus rebuked the demon, and it came out of the boy, and he was healed at that moment.
>
> Then the disciples came to Jesus in private and asked, "Why couldn't we drive it out?"
>
> He replied, "Because you have so little faith. Truly I tell you, if you have faith as small as a mustard seed, you can say to this mountain, 'Move from here to there,' and it will move. Nothing will be impossible for you."

That father knelt humbly before Jesus. This was not a whim—the man had already been pursuing men who were acknowledged followers of Christ. When that father came to Jesus with his possessed son, the stage was set for Jesus to deliver four important lessons.

1. Parents should bring requests to Jesus on behalf of their children.

2. Demons are very real and they can and must be rebuked.

3. Jesus had earlier given the disciples the ability and responsibility to cast out demons (Matthew 10:1). Clearly, they had let their gifts go dormant, and Jesus was quick to point that out. He was a bit exasperated with them: "How long shall I put up with you?" Lack of prayer and faith was probably their downfall.

4. Authentic faith moves mountains.

There's no biblical record of demons being eradicated. As a matter of fact, they appear throughout the last book of the Bible. Some scholars say that the 200 million mounted troops described in Revelation 9:16 are demons.

So, Mom and Dad, I'm recommending a preemptive strike. Pray a hedge of protection around each of your children. And if you suspect any of your precious children are already under the influence of demonic activity, pray extra hard. And recruit a small army of faithful believers to join you in prayer on a regular basis.

Prayer for Protection and Rescue from Satan

Heavenly Father. The battle is real. And Satan and his demons are stronger than any human. But when we have faith and call on your name, the victory is ours. So we pray a shield of protection—your protection—around each of our kids. Very specifically, we surrender Kayla to you. We kneel before you broken and desperate. In your name, we cast out demons. In your name, we banish Satan. In your name, we ask you to work mightily in Kayla's life. Open her eyes to every dark corner of sin she's holding onto. Show her a glimpse of light. Draw her to you. Break the chains of addiction and any demon that has a hold of her. Help us to love her. Help us to say what needs to be said. And do what needs to be done. But we know full well this battle will be lost without your intervention. Please come. Please come, Lord. We pray this in the name of your Son, Jesus. Amen.

Submit yourselves, then, to God. Resist the devil, and he will flee from you.

James 4:7

29

Pray Illegally

When I was growing up, we had a statue of St. Francis of Assisi in our backyard. I grew up Catholic and my dad was a fan. So in his honor—and because it's awesome and moving—I'm going to include the Prayer of St. Francis right here:

Lord, make me an instrument of your peace.
Where there is hatred, let me sow love;
where there is injury, pardon;
where there is doubt, faith;
where there is despair, hope;
where there is darkness, light;
and where there is sadness, joy.
O Divine Master, grant that I may not so much seek
to be consoled as to console;
to be understood as to understand;
to be loved as to love.
For it is in giving that we receive;
it is in pardoning that we are pardoned;
and it is in dying that we are born to eternal life.
Amen.

Pretty sweet, huh? You've probably seen that prayer before, but if you haven't, read it through a couple more times. Consider the idea of being an instrument of peace. Where cruddy stuff is happening, do the opposite. Live unselfishly. And know that God calls us to live in ways that are opposite of what the culture expects.

My dad even decoupaged that prayer and gave copies to his four children.

He did a lot of decoupaging. His style involved cutting out a poem, prayer, or picture and then burning the edges to make it look like old parchment. Then the actual decoupage: gluing it on a piece of flat, stained wood and slapping on ten coats of varnish. Finally he'd attach some kind of brass ring to hang it on the wall. When I was a kid, all over our house were decoupaged images of Lincoln, the Declaration of Independence, Psalms, wedding invitations, and baseball cards. When I was elected president of my senior class in college, Ken Payleitner decoupaged the article from the school newspaper, and it hung in his family room for 30 years.

My dad also brought some decoupaged pieces to work. Including the Prayer of St. Francis. Which would have been perfectly acceptable, except that he was an elementary-school principal during the era when prayer in public schools was stirring up some controversy. Not one to rock the boat, my dad did something even better. He changed a few words and hung that prayer just outside his office. The plaque, which remained there unchallenged for more than 20 years, went something like this:

> *Help me work for peace.*
> *Where there is hatred, let me sow love;*
> *where there is injury, pardon;*
> *where there is doubt, faith;*
> *where there is despair, hope;*
> *where there is darkness, light;*
> *and where there is sadness, joy.*
> *Help me not so much seek*
> *to be consoled as to console;*
> *to be understood as to understand;*
> *to be loved as to love.*
> *For it is in giving that we receive;*
> *it is in pardoning that we are pardoned;*
> *and when I leave this world, help me have an impact that*
> *lasts forever.*
>
> *Francis of Assisi*

Now posting something like that is only slightly controversial. And he didn't really put his job on the line or expect a lawsuit from the ACLU. But in his own way, my dad was saying that biblical principles apply to the life of every student in his building. And even if he had to bend a few rules, he wanted visitors to his office to see a version of that prayer that meant so much to him.

What's hanging in your home? What's hanging on the wall at your place of work? What prayers, biblical passages, words of wisdom are so important to you that you might pass them on for your children to hang on their walls? In a frame. On a poster. Or even decoupaged.

For some art snobs, it would be real easy to make fun of my dad's ubiquitous shellacked wooden wall hangings. But that would be their loss. Principal Kenneth Payleitner really did work for peace. And because of him, I have taken the Prayer of St. Francis to heart. It's a legacy of prayer I cherish.

Prayer for Legacy

Heavenly Father. My parents weren't perfect. And I'm not going to be a perfect parent. Help me to take the best of what my mother and father taught me and pass it on to my kids. Help me also to not pass on any part of that heritage that needs to be left behind or forgotten. Let me also work for peace. Let me be bold and public with my faith. Inspire me to leave behind tangible reminders of how God has worked in my life. And thank you, Lord, for all moms and dads who leave a legacy. We pray in the name of your Son, Jesus. Amen.

Make every effort to live in peace with everyone and to be holy; without holiness no one will see the Lord.

Hebrews 12:14

30

Pray Straw into the Manger

The idea was well conceived and sincerely motivated. However, when it came to execution, the four Payleitner kids were acting more like the apathetic innkeeper than the welcoming shepherds. Let me explain.

Once upon a time my mom and dad had a marvelous idea to help their children prepare their hearts for Christmas. Right after Thanksgiving, we set up the Nativity scene in its traditional spot on the mantel above the fireplace. Except this year we left out one of the little figurines. The plan was for Jesus to be gently placed there on Christmas morning, lovingly cradled by a manger filled with tiny pieces of straw that Mary Kay, Mark, Jay, and Susan would earn over the five weeks of Advent.

It didn't happen. We were supposed to prepare our hearts for the baby Jesus through daily prayer and good deeds. Thirty days times four kids should have added up to at least 120 pieces of straw. Right? As memory serves, the four of us either lost focus or didn't capture the vision. Heading toward Christmas Eve, there were fewer than a dozen pieces of straw in the little ceramic feed trough. My mom and dad didn't want to turn a sweet idea into a burdensome guilt trip, so one night a few days before Christmas, baby Jesus just appeared and not much else was said.

Some might consider the "make-a-comfy-bed-for-baby-Jesus" experiment a failure. But I don't. Just the fact that my parents presented the idea is a good thing. I don't remember if my older sister or brother rolled their eyes at the family project, but even if they did there's still a solid takeaway that Jesus is the reason for the season. I do remember feeling a little bad for not following through. And that's not a bad thing either. Nine-year-old boys need to develop a conscience that nudges them once in a while with the thought, *Hey, you dropped the ball on this one.*

One other obvious benefit has emerged years later: My parents' staw-in-the-manger experiment morphed into a chapter in this book that includes a few worthwhile thoughts on parenting and creative prayer. So here goes:

1. Go ahead and follow through on your best creative ideas to advance your kids' spiritual growth. Object lessons really connect with some children. At Christmas, pass out candy canes and talk about the shepherd's crook, the hard candy representing Jesus the rock, and the red stripes depicting the blood he shed for us. On a nature walk, pick a three-leaf clover to help describe the Trinity or chase a butterfly while talking about how a caterpillar is "born again" during metamorphosis in the cocoon. Play a whispering game that prompts your kids to walk closer and closer to each other, then explain James 4:8, which promises, "Come near to God and he will come near to you."

2. Don't beat yourself up when you dive enthusiastically into a new round of daily family devotions and the rest of your crew doesn't share your excitement. You're planting seeds. Some grow, some don't. You're advancing the idea that connecting to God needs to be intentional. Kids will remember that. You're learning what works and what doesn't. So next time your family devotions will last for three months, rather than three days. And of course you never really know when a single, simple truth penetrates a child's mind and heart. A sincere thought-provoking activity might be life-changing for any child at any age. You may not know the importance of that instant for many years. Indeed, you may never know.

3. Don't forget you have to give the Holy Spirit a little room to work. Yes, we need to be creative, diligent, and intentional about praying with and for our kids. But our human limitations keep us from knowing the best way to pray. The Bible reminds us, "The Spirit helps us in our weakness. We do not know what we ought to pray for, but the Spirit himself intercedes for us through wordless groans" (Romans 8:26).

So, Mom and Dad, I totally encourage you to fearlessly launch innovative prayer projects and devotions with your children with enthusiasm and high expectations. You may even want to invest in an activity set called "The Good Deed Manger," which includes the cutest little stuffed donkey, a charming storybook, a manger, a swaddled baby Jesus, and a few dozen felt strips of "hay."

If your creative efforts yield new spiritual insights for your family, share your successes with other friends and families. If you end up with uninspired kids and an empty manger, don't spend too much time judging or regretting your efforts. You just never know. God uses all of it.

Prayer for Creativity As You Parent

Heavenly Father. Help us to use the gift of creativity to connect with our kids. And to connect them with you. Also, help us to be patient with our children, ourselves, and your timing. We know you work all things for good. We promise to give our best efforts. We ask you to bless our work on your behalf—even when we fall way, way short of perfection. We pray in the name of your Son, Jesus. Amen.

When Joseph and Mary had done everything required by the Law of the Lord, they returned to Galilee to their own town of Nazareth. And the child grew and became strong; he was filled with wisdom, and the grace of God was on him.

Luke 2:39-40

31

Pray They Are Not Scared
of the Holy Ghost

All kids have visual images in their head of God and Jesus that come out of some artist's imagination. There's the Sistine Chapel God and the image of God wielding a bolt of lightning. There's the soft pastel smiling Jesus, the baby-in-a-manger-with-a-halo Jesus, and some images of Jesus on the cross that might be terrifying to young children.

Of course, the visual artists' interpretation of what God looks like is just that, an interpretation. Something dreamed up by the painter or sculptor. John 1:18 declares, "No one has ever seen God." If you think about it for a moment, you realize we don't really know what Jesus looks like either. There are no photos or even paintings by first-century artists. The Bible doesn't really describe what he looked like. Of course, any actor they find to portray Jesus on film is going to be handsome. I have no problem with that.

The third member of the Trinity doesn't have that kind of image problem. At one time the term *Holy Ghost* may have frightened small children. But that expression went out with the idea that Satan has horns and carries a pitchfork. The Holy Spirit is actually well-described in Scripture. We know what he looks like. (Or at least what forms he can take.) He is like a dove. Like fire. Like a river. He sounds like a rushing wind.

As soon as Jesus was baptized, he went up out of the water. At that moment heaven was opened, and he saw the Spirit of God descending like a dove and alighting on him (Matthew 3:16).

They saw what seemed to be tongues of fire that separated and came to rest on each of them. All of them were filled with the Holy Spirit (Acts 2:3-4).

"Whoever believes in me, as Scripture has said, rivers of living water will flow from within them." By this he [Jesus] meant the Spirit, whom those who believed in him were later to receive (John 7:38-39).

When the day of Pentecost came, they were all together in one place. Suddenly a sound like the blowing of a violent wind came from heaven and filled the whole house where they were sitting (Acts 2:1-2).

A dove, fire, living water, wind. I hope those are comforting images to you. Because the Holy Spirit is the Person of the Trinity who supernaturally bears gifts and guidance for all believers. He was sent not just to walk beside mankind as Jesus did, but to guide us from within.

Don't you know that you yourselves are God's temple and that God's Spirit dwells in your midst? (1 Corinthians 3:16).

So much happened on the night of the Last Supper that it's easy to miss the critical announcement by Jesus about the Holy Spirit. The apostles were probably shocked that Jesus was leaving, but he promised, "I will not leave you as orphans" (John 14:18) right after he had promised to send "another advocate [Counselor]" (John 14:16). Imagine their confusion! Another counselor? How could anyone possibly replace Jesus, their living, breathing, walking friend who had taught them with such clarity? Jesus calmed their fears.

"Very truly I tell you, it is for your good that I am going away. Unless I go away, the Advocate will not come to you; but if I go, I will send him to you. When he comes, he will prove the

world to be in the wrong about sin and righteousness and judg-
ment" (John 16:7-8).

The second chapter of Acts records the promised coming of the
Holy Spirit, and Christians have been blessed by his supernatural presence ever since. One of the most compelling gifts of the Spirit is that
he takes the worry out of defending our faith and delivering our personal testimony. Jesus taught,

> *"Do not worry about how you will defend yourselves or what*
> *you will say, for the Holy Spirit will teach you at that time*
> *what you should say" (Luke 12:11-12).*

The Spirit also helps us pray. For our kids and with our kids. Even
when we don't know what's best for our family or even how to pray, he
will give us peace in our prayer life. As we read in the previous chapter…

> *The Spirit helps us in our weakness. We do not know what*
> *we ought to pray for, but the Spirit himself intercedes for us*
> *through wordless groans (Romans 8:26).*

Mom and Dad, keep praying with your kids about all their decisions. If they have not yet reached the age of reason, take the stress away
by making major decisions for them. As soon as possible, though, help
them learn to listen for the leadings of the Holy Spirit within. Stick
around and make yourself available to be a clarifying influence and
sounding board, but give your kids plenty of room to practice and
hone the skill of decision making. They need to be able to discern
right from wrong and better from best. For their first thousand choices,
they're going to need you as their safety net. And even when they stop
asking for your guidance, keep praying.

Prayer for a Spirit-Led Life

Heavenly Father. We understand the Trinity as one God in three persons. You, the Father, in heaven. Your Son, Jesus, who came to earth and will come again. And the Holy Spirit, who this moment is revealing the best plan for our life. A plan designed by You. Which began when we accepted Christ as our Savior. We don't have everything figured out and that's okay. We do pray we can fully appreciate and utilize the fruit off the Spirit and listen to his quiet voice as it leads us this very day. In the name of the Father, the Son, and the Holy Spirit. Amen.

The fruit of the Spirit is love, joy, peace, patience, kindness, goodness, faithfulness, gentleness, self-control.

Galatians 5:22-23 NASB

32

Pray for a Lost Wallet

True story. The Payleitner minivan was one of five vehicles driving from the western suburbs of Chicago, through the northwest corner of Indiana, just into Michigan, destined for Warren Dunes State Park. The one-day trip was a summer tradition with the Strattons, Beehs, Sjostroms, Clausens, Breedens, our dear friend Hildred, and anyone else who tagged along for a day at the beach. I was driving, Rita was copilot, and I don't remember who was in the back because the kids all jumped in different vans.

On the way, the caravan always pulled in at the Michigan Welcome Center in New Buffalo on I-94 for one last pit stop. Six hours later, after romping and sun-soaking all day on beautiful Lake Michigan, the entire group of some 30 adults and kids would stop for burgers at the famed Redamak's in New Buffalo. You don't mess with tradition.

Rolling into the park entrance, I reached for my wallet to pay the five-dollar visitor's fee. The wallet wasn't in my pocket. And I instantly knew what had happened. For driving comfort, I had pulled out my wallet and tossed it on the dashboard. When we had stopped at the welcome center, we had all piled out of the minivan to stretch our legs, use the restrooms, and grab a travel brochure or two. Without thinking, we left all the doors and windows open. Someone either looking for an easy target or just happening to walk by saw the wallet through the windshield and grabbed it. It was an easy, two-second heist. Whoever it was, I almost can't blame them. I had made it too tempting.

Anyway. I dropped my van load of beach bums at the park and drove the ten miles back to the welcome center. My first stop was the information desk, where the very nice attendant said, "Sorry, no one's turned in a lost wallet." With that discouraging news, I tried to think like a wallet thief. Of course they wouldn't want to keep the wallet— they would probably grab the cash and credit cards and toss it, right? I searched the parking lot. I sifted through the garbage cans. I walked a quarter-mile down the highway shoulder, imagining some punk tossing my wallet out the window of his speeding car. I did everything humanly possible to regain possession of my wallet.

Stopping at the benches outside the center, I paused again to consider my options. The contents of the wallet flashed through my head: driver's license, irreplaceable photos, library card, credit cards. What a hassle. Should I contact the Michigan State Police? What could they do anyway? I also didn't want to ruin the day for everyone. I thought of everything. But I hadn't thought of God.

I chuckled at myself. These were all friends from church. Knowing these families, I realized they were probably praying for me. Something I had not done. So I did. I prayed, "God, help me find my wallet."

Ten seconds later the nice attendant from the information desk walked out and said, "Is this it? Someone just turned it in."

I chuckled again. "Yeah, it is. Thanks." The only thing missing was the cash. Phew.

Back at the dunes, it was confirmed that word had spread through the entire group and every member of the caravan had indeed been praying. Except me. I was so busy trying to think like a wallet thief that I didn't think like a Christian. When I told my story of prayer being answered, they loved it. But no one was surprised.

The day was saved. The Payleitner family and friends had another great day at Warren Dunes. Later, at Redamak's, the other families chipped in to pick up our dinner tab plus tip. About $85. The wallet thief had taken $80. Which meant I came out ahead. And when I think about that lesson on the power of prayer, we all came out way, way ahead.

Prayer That Turns to God First

Heavenly Father. I'm stuck. I'm in a tight spot. A difficult situation. And my first instinct is to figure a way out myself. Thank you for my common sense, my intellect, my creativity, and all my problem-solving skills. They are a gift from you. But Lord, I'm coming to you first. No matter what happens, I know you will take care of me. I trust you with every moment of my life. The easy times. And the tough times. I pray in the name of your Son, Jesus. Amen.

"Seek first His kingdom and His righteousness, and all these things will be added to you."

Jesus, in Matthew 6:33 NASB

33

Pray Using Names

Our church had finally hired a full-time youth pastor. Frank, a fresh graduate of Wheaton College, had an entire summer to prepare for the upcoming school year. You might think the priorities of such a task were obvious. Things like getting to know the rest of the ministry staff, preparing curriculum, recruiting volunteers, and planning a smashing event to kick off the ministry year.

Frank did all that. But he identified and executed another task that was much more critical. He gathered the names of every high-schooler who was connected in any way to our church and he prayed. He prayed for each of them by name, every day, for the entire summer.

What did that accomplish? Those prayers softened Frank's heart for each of those young people. Also, without their even knowing it, the heart of each of those students was also being prepared to hear the gospel and biblical truth they all desperately needed. And who knows? Those heartfelt prayers that summer may have helped more than one teen deal effectively with a personal crisis or difficult decision. Frank's prayers may have prevented one parent from losing their cool and kicking their son out of the house after a two-way screaming match that got out of hand. That summer of intentional prayer may have prevented one kid from drinking, one kid from smoking pot, and one young couple from giving into temptation and losing their virginity. That's all very possible.

Later that fall and winter, I personally talked with quite a few students who were totally surprised about how active they had become in a church youth group. They told me they just happened to have nothing to do on the evening of the end-of-summer youth group kickoff event. So they wandered over. And they felt welcome. And it wasn't terrible. So they came back. And they got curious about Jesus. I give full credit to God's responding favorably to Frank's persistent prayer.

I believe that's how God works. He calls us to pray. Especially for others. Ephesians 6:18 instructs us,

> Pray in the Spirit on all occasions with all kinds of prayers and requests. With this in mind, be alert and always keep on praying for all the Lord's people.

But let's not forget one element to Frank's summer prayer project that sealed the deal. He prayed for these young people by name. Eric. Becky. Brian. Brad. Amy. Sarah. Tony. Sheila. One by one. Over and over. He prayed through that list of more than 150 names all summer long. These were names of real kids with real needs.

In the Parable of the Good Shepherd, the sheep know Jesus' voice. That's not surprising. But what is surprising is that he calls them by name.

> "The one who enters by the gate is the shepherd of the sheep. The gatekeeper opens the gate for him, and the sheep listen to his voice. He calls his own sheep by name and leads them out" (John 10:2-3).

Do sheep have names? Really? In any case, your children have names. But do you pray for them by name? Do you lift them up as individuals? That's part of helping them discover their own unique gifts and talents. Picture each face. Imagine where they are this very minute. Snug in their beds. Playing video games at a friend's house. In a dorm room. Driving to Denver. Tucking their own kids in bed. Stop right now and pray that God holds them in the palm of his hand. You can't always know what's going on in their heads. You won't know the opportunities and dangers just around the next corner. But God knows. And he's waiting for your prayers.

Then, Mom and Dad, take it a step further. Pray for your children's *friends* by name. Those boys and girls—young men and young ladies— have a tremendous impact on the lives of your kids. Praying for them by name might be one of the wisest things you ever do. If you can't name at least a couple of friends for each of your kids, shame on you. Commit to identifying those friends ASAP. As a matter of fact, let's make that an assignment before you turn to the next chapter.

Finally, I may not know your name, but if you track me down on my website, I'll be glad to add your name to my prayer list. I'm hoping you'll do the same for me.

Prayer That Names Names

Heavenly Father. I pray for Alec, Lindsay, Randall, Rachel, Max, Megan, Isaac, Kaitlin, and Rae Anne. And my kids' friends, Reed, Bryan, Ryan, Kyle, and Ali. In the name of Jesus. Amen.

Do not fear, for I have redeemed you;
I have summoned you by name; you are mine.

Isaiah 43:1

34

Pray Submissive Prayers

When I was a new Christian, I stumbled across the secret formula for answered prayer. So I thought.

All I had to do was connect two unrelated verses from the first book of the New Testament. Matthew 21:22 clearly promises, "If you believe, you will receive whatever you ask for in prayer." Matthew 6:9 clearly instructs us, "This, then, is how you should pray." As mentioned in chapter 17, that instruction is immediately followed by what has come to be known as the Lord's Prayer.

Of course, I thought I was the only person on the planet who had discovered how these two portions of Scripture might actually be the formula for filling our every need. Put them together and *shazam*! Pray the *right* way and you get *everything* you ask for.

Well, it turns out my secret formula was not so secret. Anyone who had been listening and studying God's Word for any length of time knew those verses well. And the smart ones knew they did not consti-tute a magic formula. The problem was, I had applied my own selfish Bible interpretation on behalf of my own selfish little world. I needed a serious lesson in big-picture thinking.

The best way to get a handle on big-picture thinking is to read and meditate on Romans 8:28. "We know that in all things God works for the good of those who love him, who have been called according to his purpose." Now if you've suffered a recent tragedy, that's not an easy portion of Scripture to read. I recommend you turn to words describing God's comfort. Psalm 46 and 116 come to mind.

In severe pain or grief, you may not be able to imagine any possible way that God can take your suffering and have it "work for the good." But the truth is, he promises to do exactly that. The challenge for most of us is that the "good" may not be clear to us right away. As a matter of fact, God promises that for the time being he very likely *won't* make his ways clear. Paul writes,

> *Now we see things imperfectly, like puzzling reflections in a mirror, but then we will see everything with perfect clarity. All that I know now is partial and incomplete, but then I will know everything completely, just as God now knows me completely (1 Corinthians 13:12 NLT).*

Another way to define and embrace big-picture thinking is to look at the most difficult decision or conflict you face and pray the same words Jesus spoke in the Garden of Gethsemane: "Not my will, but yours be done" (Luke 22:42). The author of Hebrews reflects on the many times Jesus submitted to the will of his Father.

> *During the days of Jesus' life on earth, he offered up prayers and petitions with fervent cries and tears to the one who could save him from death, and he was heard because of his reverent submission. Son though he was, he learned obedience from what he suffered (Hebrews 5:7-8).*

That kind of submission is especially difficult for loving parents who have high aspirations for their children. An expectant couple shares a vision of their newborn grabbing their fingers—their baby's first smiles, first steps, first words, not to mention sandcastles, bike rides, ball games, graduations, and future generations. But it doesn't always happen that way. Acclaimed author and speaker Nancy Guthrie explains what it's like to cry out to God in brokenness.

> Several years ago, physicians told my husband and me that because of a rare metabolic disorder, our newborn

daughter, Hope, would live for only two or three months. Time seemed to be slipping away so quickly when one day, as I rocked Hope in the nursery we'd prepared for her—tears spilling down my face—I thought, *I'll ask God to give Hope more time.* It seemed such a modest prayer; I'd already surrendered any insistence that God heal her completely. But even as that prayer formed in my mind, I sensed God calling me to submit to his perfect timing. So my prayer instead became, *Give me strength to make the most of every day you give me with Hope. Show me how to rest in your plan for her life and mine.*[4]

Why does God allow some kids to be healthy and others not? Why does one family seem to cruise through life while their neighbors experience crisis after crisis? We can ask, but God's ways might not make any sense in this lifetime. Still, while you're waiting for an answer, it may be wise to look around and see who and what God has placed in your path. He may be equipping you to make a difference in this world in extraordinary ways this very day.

Nancy Guthrie goes on to say that submissive prayer "welcomes God to work in and through my suffering rather than begs him to take it away. It's thanking God for what he gives me rather than resenting him for what I lose."[5]

So maybe there is a secret formula for answered prayer after all. It's trusting that God knows what's best and submitting to his will for your life. And then keeping open the lines of communication. Keep asking for what you think is best for you and your family. Keep praying for needs large and small. Maybe even keep a prayer diary and confidently include a box after each prayer to check when that prayer is answered.

In the end—the very end—don't be surprised if you get everything you ask for.

Prayer That His Will Be Done

Heavenly Father. I submit to your will for my life. I submit my entire family to your will. Help me accept and even celebrate every twist and turn in my life. Help me to look for ways that you can use me to answer the prayer of others. Your will be done. In the name of Jesus. Amen.

Rejoice always, pray continually, give thanks in all circumstances; for this is God's will for you in Christ Jesus.

1 Thessalonians 5:16-18

35

Pray Your Own Prayer Requests with Your Kids

If your four-year-old is into dinosaurs, you be into dinosaurs.

Long ago, I know you learned how to identify a stegosaurus and T-rex. And that knowledge is critical for any parent of a preschooler. But did you know that the largest dinosaur to ever roam the earth is *not* the brontosaurus? Despite the fact that Fred Flintstone regularly dined on bronto burgers, it turns out that overenthusiastic nineteenth-century paleontologists slapped together the bones of a couple different skeletons and invented a creature that never existed. The answer to the question about the largest land animal that ever lived is "Argentinosaurus."

If your eight-year-old daughter is into American Girls, you be into American Girls.

You'll need to keep your credit card loaded. And be ready to say no to some of her requests. But there really is something sweet about a girl playing with dolls which represent different eras of American history. Read the books with her. Do the puzzles and activities. Best of all, you'll know exactly what to get her for her birthday and Christmas. That is, until she tires of AG and moves on to the next phase of life.

If your 13-year-old is into skateboards, you be into skateboards.

It may not be something you fully appreciate, but go ahead and watch him work on his kick flip or backside 50-50 at the local skate parks. Make the two-hour drive to that really cool skateboard store. It may be a phase. It may be a lifetime hobby. He will be glad you were there. And so will you.

So much of parenting is about entering their world. You are learning what makes them tick, how they learn, and what motivates them. That's all valuable information to have as you go before them, stand next to them, and send them off on their own.

The flipside of that is inviting them to enter *your* world. That's one of the ways your children learn responsibility, perseverance, and how to make adult decisions.

Your kids don't have to know all your financial doings, but they should know that you have a budget and sometimes have to say no to the things you'd really like to have or really like to do.

Your kids should have an idea of what you do for a living. When my son Max was seven I spent a lot of time in my office just off the kitchen writing scripts, designing ads, and coordinating radio-production schedules. Between tasks I'd stretch my legs or grab a snack. I overheard him tell a friend once that "my dad's job is eating apples."

Your kids need to know that if something happened to you, their needs will be taken care of by a life-insurance policy you pay for. But you probably don't want to tell them the amount of the death benefit. For a variety of reasons.

One of the best ways for your kids to enter your world is to ask them to pray with you and for you. It's a win-win-win. You pray. They pray. God listens and his heart is moved.

Choose the right issues to pray about. Don't put pressure on your young children to help make any adult decisions. Don't outline details of adult situations that are too complex for their brains to handle. And don't reveal secrets you don't want broadcast around the neighborhood or schoolyard. But do ask them to pray for you and with you.

Pray about any new career opportunities. Tell them the pluses and minuses. A few more dollars vs. longer hours away from the family.

Pray about whether you should get a new furnace or new roof. You want to be a good steward with your money and your home. Those kinds of decisions are very tangible examples of occasions in which you want God's guidance.

Pray about a friend or colleague who is facing a life-threatening illness, marital crisis, or rebellious teenager. You don't have to give names or specifics. God knows all the details anyway. Also make it clear that you're not talking about yourself.

One excellent area to pray about with your child is your family's end-of-the-year gift. Should you give a chunk of money to a ministry endorsed by your church? Or a charity that has a special meaning to your family? Something local where you are making a difference in your own community? Or is it more meaningful to support a mission outreach on the other side of the world and trust God to use your gift for his glory? Explain the options and, without trying to sway their opinions, turn the decision over to God.

One parenting note: again, you may not want to give too much information to your kids. If you talk about specific amounts, that may come back to bite you. A teenager might say, "Oh fine, you can give $500 to dig wells in Africa, but you can't give me $20 for pizza with my friends."

Inviting your kids to enter your world and then praying for some of the things on your heart has all kinds of bonus benefits. It helps your kids realize they are not the center of the universe. It gives them a smidge of understanding when they ask you a question and your mind is elsewhere. And it clues them in on what's ahead for the family.

But don't ask your kids to pray with you for any of those reasons. Ask them to pray because prayer changes things. God listens. God's heart is moved. God heals. God opens doors. God brings clarity when we face difficult decisions.

Ask your kids to pray for you. That's a powerful strategy for bringing families together.

Prayer for Yourself

Heavenly Father. You know about the reorganization at the office. I pray for wisdom for those in charge and that the right people are put in the right positions. I ask that you help me be salt and light wherever I fit in the company plans. For Mr. Benchley's surgery next week. We pray it goes well and for a quick recovery. And that his family surrounds him with love and support. Lord, I'm trying to decide what to do about the plumbing in the upstairs bathroom. Can you help us decide? I know it's not a life-changing issue, but we're stumped. For this family. My great marriage. Our kids. Especially Zachary here. Praying alongside him is a privilege. If it's your will, we ask you to keep the blessings coming. Help us turn to you and trust you for all our needs big and small. We pray in the name of Jesus. Amen.

"Where two or three gather in my name, there am I with them."

Jesus, in Matthew 18:20

36

Pray for Your Church

Young kids know that "church" is a big deal. Mom and dad talk about it and fuss about it all the time. An English professor would be delighted at the large number of prepositions we use to precede the word *church*.

Right out loud, we wonder what's going on *at* church. We can't wait to try the new restaurant opening up *by* church. We call Dennis and Mary our friends *from* church. We ask new friends, "Where do you go *to* church?" And of course, we do things *after* church.

We may not get all dressed up in our Sunday finest like they did generations ago, but moms still put a little extra effort into what kids are wearing *for* church. And, we get a little defensive when someone has something *against* church, especially our church.

We talk *about* church a lot. Often, when our kids hear us there's a sense of urgency about it. Maybe even a twinge of negativity.

"Remember we've got church tomorrow!"

"I wish I could, but we're going to church."

"We're late for church."

For busy families, the backlash of scrambling to get ready for church typically lasts well into the church service itself. Author and blogger John Acuff says, "The hour before you attend church is like the devil's Super Bowl."[6] On his website StuffChristiansLike.net, Acuff identifies with millions of churchgoing parents when he recalls the weekly Sunday morning challenge of finding the kids' shoes, putting those shoes on the kids' feet, and then manhandling all the kids, all their feet, and all their shoes into the car.

I hope you love your church. And you probably do. Whatever denomination, size, schedule, or worship style, I'm hoping it meets your exact needs. I trust there's a place for your children to grow in the knowledge and love of the Father, the Son, and the Holy Spirit. I hope there's a chance to serve within the church walls (if your church has walls), impact your community, and reach out to others in and around the world.

But what vibe are you sending out to your kids? Do they know you love the church? Not just the building, of course, but the people—pastors, secretaries, volunteers, janitors, worship leaders, and every individual in every pew (or whatever you sit in). You want your children to feel good about those people and that place.

You can and should have long, thoughtful conversations about your church with your spouse. Talk about the good stuff and not-so-good stuff. But don't torch your church in front of the kids. Extinguish any harsh criticism before you and your family get burnt. Of course, a give-and-take discussion with a teenager about what's going on at youth group doesn't have to be all roses and daffodils. Every church youth program in the country is going to have its share of drama. But even that conversation should end on a hopeful note.

Want your kids to love church? Consider these three suggestions:

1. Lay out clothes (including shoes) the night before and start setting your alarm 15 minutes earlier.
2. Intentionally notice the nice things going on at church and point them out.
3. Pray with your kids for your church.

Pray for the staff and their families. Pray for special events. Pray for new believers. Pray for the specific programs in which you may be involved. Pray for those ministries that you and your kids may not typically notice, like meals for shut-ins, marital counseling, pregnancy resource centers, AA meetings, and support of local homeless shelters. Your kids will start seeing your church in a whole new way, as a light-house for the community. And they may want to get involved.

Often, prayer needs to be simply prayer. But when it comes to ministry opportunities initiated by your church, go ahead and begin to suggest your older kids volunteer in areas that match their gifts and passions. Your prayer time can lead directly to hands-on ministry.

Praying for a church body is a long-standing Christian tradition. Flip through the opening paragraphs of Paul's letters to the Romans, Ephesians, Philippians, Colossians, and Thessalonians. Paul, who was clearly a man of action, mentions quite specifically that he prays for these churches.

While you're praying with your kids about church, ask God how he might also use you in a surprising new way. Your conversations about church will gain a whole new sparkle.

Prayer for Ministry Opportunities

Heavenly Father. I want to be a good steward of my time. I don't want to volunteer for my own ego or out of guilt. So I'm going to trust you. Please, Lord, if there's an area of ministry or volunteering that you want me to do, make it real clear. It could be at church. It could be at Chloe's school. It could be something that is not even on my radar screen. Wherever you call me, I pray my service will reflect your love and light into the community. Protect my time with my family. But use me. I pray this and all things in the name of your Son, Jesus, who went to the cross for me. Amen.

I thank my God every time I remember you. In all my prayers for all of you, I always pray with joy because of your partnership in the gospel from the first day until now, being confident of this, that he who began a good work in you will carry it on to completion until the day of Christ Jesus.

Philippians 1:3-5

37

Pray You Have the Courage and Wisdom to Break Your Child's Plate

It was Max's first extended time away from his home in Texas. He was working out of state with his two best friends, so the summer of 1974 was supposed to be a fun and profitable three months. But the work was harder than expected and his friends quit and went back home. From a phone booth in Georgia, after midnight, the 19-year-old called home. Hearing his parents' voices made him even feel even lonelier. Max remembers,

> As I explained my plight, I could tell my mom wanted me to come home. But just as she said, "Why don't you come…" my dad, who was on the extension, interrupted her. "We'd love for you to come back, but we've already broken your plate." (That was West Texas talk for "We love you, Max, but it's time to grow up.") It takes a wise father to know when to push his son out of the nest. It's painful, but it has to be done. I'll always be thankful that my dad gave me wings and then made me use them.

Max's father was an oil-field worker. His mother was a nurse. (Doesn't that sound about right?) And that young man grew up to be one of the most respected and best-loved pastors and storytellers of our era.

Max Lucado tells that story in his book *On the Anvil* not for sympathy. Not to instruct parents how to exhibit tough love. And not just to thank his father. I believe that story resonates because most parents everywhere will always struggle with that same issue. Balancing when to say, "Come home," and when to say, "Time to grow up." When to rescue and when to let them take responsibility for their choices.

Can you look back on a moment in your life and say, "That's when I really became an adult"? It was probably in your late teens or early twenties. But think back and really consider the circumstances. You didn't become an adult when you earned your first paycheck, but when your boss gave you some real responsibility. It wasn't the day you signed with the army recruiter, but the night you bedded down after a brutal day at basic training and realized, "I can do this." You didn't instantly grow up the day your parents dropped you off at college, but you took a big step toward maturity the night you said no to getting drunk with the other freshmen.

Isn't that what you want for your kids? Adults make adult decisions. And our goal is to raise responsible adults.

It wasn't easy for Max Lucado's mom and dad to let him travel three states away for summer employment. And don't kid yourself, that decision was just as difficult for Dad as it was for Mom. Dad was the one who said, "We've already broken your plate." But that father also knew the kind of temptations and trouble a 19-year-old boy will experience with pals during the course of a long, hot summer.

Max Lucado's life-changing summer was more than four decades ago. These days a lot of young people don't get their plates broken and get pushed out of the nest until they're well into their twenties. Which is especially confusing because many of those same young people have been pretending they were adults since before they were teenagers. Girls wearing makeup and dressing like adults in grade school. Boys watching pornography on their smart phones on the middle-school playground.

It's enough to drive parents to their knees.

Prayer for Maturity

Heavenly Father. We lift up Madeline and Jayden. They're just kids. They have so much to learn. In this world, you will provide many wonderful opportunities where they can test and stretch themselves in order to become independent thinkers and doers. But we know there are also many dangers and temptations that can damage or destroy them. Please guide them, protect them, provide for them. Help them grow up, but not too fast. And not too slow. As their parents, we trust you. Help us parent our younger children with consistency and conviction. Help us parent our older children with courage and wisdom. And always with love, grace, and hearts surrendered to you. We pray in the name of your Son, Jesus. Amen.

When I was a child, I talked like a child, I thought like a child, I reasoned like a child. When I became a man, I put the ways of childhood behind me.

1 Corinthians 13:11

38

Pray Out Your Anger

In his book, *Prayer: Does It Make Any Difference?*, Philip Yancey opens up one chapter describing an unforgettable moment he experienced at the church he attends. In a typical weekend service, time would be set aside for people in the pews to voice aloud their prayers. Yancey describes most of the prayers he has heard over the years as polite. But one prayer stands out because of its raw emotion:

> In a clear but wavering voice a young woman began with the words, "God, I hated you after the rape! How could you let this happen to me?" The congregation abruptly fell silent. No more rustling of papers or shifting in the seats. "And I hated the people in this church who tried to comfort me. I didn't want comfort. I wanted revenge. I wanted to hurt back. I thank you, God, that you didn't give up on me, and neither did some of these people. You kept after me, and I come back to you now and ask that you heal the scars in my soul."[7]

I hope that scene jars you a bit. And I hope you applaud that young woman. That was a prayer that needed to be prayed and needed to be heard. The others in church that day got a lesson in prayer. And you know God heard her appeal.

In his book, Yancey goes on to compare that emotional outcry to an Old Testament dialogue between God and Abraham. In Genesis

18:23-33, God had just announced the wicked cities of Sodom and Gomorrah were to be judged and Abraham responded by launching into a kind of audacious bargaining session:

> Abraham approached him and said: "Will you sweep away the righteous with the wicked? What if there are fifty righteous people in the city? Will you really sweep it away and not spare the place for the sake of the fifty righteous people in it? Far be it from you to do such a thing—to kill the righteous with the wicked, treating the righteous and the wicked alike. Far be it from you! Will not the Judge of all the earth do right?"

> The LORD said, "If I find fifty righteous people in the city of Sodom, I will spare the whole place for their sake."

> Then Abraham spoke up again: "Now that I have been so bold as to speak to the LORD, though I am nothing but dust and ashes, what if the number of the righteous is five less than fifty? Will you destroy the whole city for lack of five people?"

> "If I find forty-five there," he said, "I will not destroy it."

> Once again he spoke to him, "What if only forty are found there?"

> He said, "For the sake of forty, I will not do it."

> Then he said, "May the LORD not be angry, but let me speak. What if only thirty can be found there?"

> He answered, "I will not do it if I find thirty there."

> Abraham said, "Now that I have been so bold as to speak to the LORD, what if only twenty can be found there?"

> He said, "For the sake of twenty, I will not destroy it."

> Then he said, "May the LORD not be angry, but let me speak just once more. What if only ten can be found there?"

> He answered, "For the sake of ten, I will not destroy it."

When the LORD had finished speaking with Abraham, he left,
and Abraham returned home.

Respect. Persistence. Specificity. Boldness. Honesty. Those are attributes that should run deep in our prayers. You can't help noticing that God responded to Abraham with patience and mercy.

Sin offends God. Denying that he exists or eliminating all channels of communication with him are dangerous choices. But honest emotions from a heart open to his plan are exactly what he wants.

A hospice chaplain tells the story of a patient in the final stages of cancer who spends an entire night ranting and cursing God. The next morning, he is broken by his guilt, and he fears God can never forgive him after he displayed so much hate the night before. The chaplain knows the heart of the patient. And knows the pain and anguish that led up to the previous night's outbreak. He asks, "What do you think is the opposite of love?" The distraught patient gives the obvious answer, "Hate." The chaplain smiles gently and replies, "No, the opposite of love is indifference. Last night you were being honest with God. If you were indifferent to him you would never have spent the night engaging him like that. Actually, theologians have a word for what you were doing last night. They call it 'prayer.'"

When you pray with your kids and for your kids, be honest with yourself. And be honest with God. If that means you pray in anger, so be it. If your prayers turn into pleading, shouting, dancing, weeping, or surrendering, it's all good. He doesn't even mind if you whine, pout, rage, or attempt to bargain with him. He's big enough to handle anything you can dish out. Just don't be indifferent.

Prayer for Authenticity

Heavenly Father. If you're real, I want to know you. And I want to be real with you. No fake prayers. No wishy-washy words. No holding back anything. I want to talk to you like a friend. I want to talk to you as the Almighty Creator of the universe. I want to talk honestly. Please help me listen for your clear guidance. In Jesus' name. Amen.

The Lord is far from the wicked,
  but he hears the prayer of the righteous.

Proverbs 15:29

39

Pray for Peer Evangelism
(But Don't Call It That!)

Wish your kids had more Christian friends? There's one sure way to be proactive in that quest.

Consider Rosa. Born into a Communist Cuban home in 1985, her story is told in the compelling book *Jesus Freaks: Revolutionaries*. For years, Rosa lived under the strict atheism of parents who were loyal to Fidel Castro. But her great-grandmother secretly shared God's love with Rosa. The seeds of faith planted by the old woman—cultivated through prayer—came to harvest when Rosa received Christ as a young teenager. She secretly began reading Scripture and attending church. Ashamed of their daughter, Rosa's parents sent her to a boarding school where she would be far from the influence of other Christians. But Rosa did the same thing she had seen her great-grandmother do. She prayed for the classmates at her new school and lovingly shared the gospel. Very soon, Rosa had three Christian friends. She writes, "We meet under a tree, hidden, to share God's Word. We feel the presence of the Lord in a special way. We keep sowing and waiting that soon we will be many."[8]

Maybe—like Rosa—your kids can literally help turn their current group of non-Christian friends into Christian friends. That almost sounds impossible, doesn't it? But isn't that what we're called to do as Christians? And might peer evangelism be the best way to reach the next generation for Christ? And even if the motivation is a bit self-serving, wouldn't you like to see God work in the life of your child in such a way that they eagerly share the Good News with their friends?

On one hand, this is no small task. You will have to count on the Holy Spirit working in the lives of these young people. But you have a part to play as well. And it's really not that difficult.

As part of your regular prayer time with your own child, simply pray for their friends by name. Pray specifically that God protects them, reveals his love to them, and draws those friends to himself. You might even pray that God uses your son or daughter as a positive influence in the life of their friends. But here's the key. When you're praying or talking with your children, don't use the words *peer evangelism*.

Calling it *peer evangelism* (or *friendship evangelism*) makes it sound like their friend is a project. And your child will want no part of that. But to you as a parent, the spiritual welfare of your children and their friends really is a project. A project worth taking on. In private, pray fiercely for God to enter the lives of your children's friends, classmates, co-workers, lab partners, teammates, prom dates, and roommates. The more names you know, the better. The more prayer, the better. And you can certainly pray that your entire family will reflect biblical values to other families and the young people in your community. But you'll want to leave most of the one-on-one interaction up to your children.

If one of your daughter's classmates is sitting at your kitchen table and asks about a verse that's on your refrigerator, answer with quiet enthusiasm and a tiny bit of personal application. If one of your son's friends mentions a sick uncle, you can certainly promise to say a prayer on his behalf. But really, if your daughter or son is up for it, let them take the lead when it comes to their friend's spiritual curiosity and growth.

When you find yourself praying with your kids for their peers, keep it simple, sincere, and straightforward. Just open the door and let your son or daughter lead the way. By remembering and mentioning the names of their friends before the Creator—praying for their health and welfare—your child will very likely begin to realize that God wants to be involved in the lives of their entire circle of friends. That's a good thing.

A word of warning. Too often, spoken prayers from a parent spend way too much time outlining the problem and giving God a lot of not-so-helpful guidance on how he should answer the prayer. Mom and Dad, that's not necessary and might possibly throw up a future roadblock for your kids. You can be sure God already knows the problem and has a much better solution than any you could ever think of. Plus, hearing extensive specifics in your long-winded prayer may lead your own off-spring to regret having shared so many details with you. Also, if you cover all the bases in your prayers for Lily, Kyra, or Tyler, there's no room for your child to add their own prayer concerns. Make sense?

Gently guiding and inspiring your children to become peer evangelists may be one of the most fulfilling and valuable things you ever do. And like so many worthwhile endeavors, it starts with prayer.

Prayer for Your Friends (and Theirs)

Heavenly Father. You know how so many of my friends seem to be going through a tough time right now. Kathy and Tom worrying about their son in college. Diane seeing her mother go through Alzheimer's. The Nelsons and the O'Keefes. Any action you want me to take, please make it clear. I would be honored to come alongside these friends in crisis, but I don't want to be intrusive. Help me be the right kind of friend. And I also pray for Olivia's friends. Especially Lily and Kyra. And Tyler. These are great kids. Thank you that they are in Olivia's life. And vice versa. Please keep all these young people close to you. We love and trust you. In Jesus' name. Amen.

In your hearts revere Christ as Lord. Always be prepared to give an answer to everyone who asks you to give the reason for the hope that you have. But do this with gentleness and respect, keeping a clear conscience, so that those who speak maliciously against your good behavior in Christ may be ashamed of their slander.

1 Peter 3:15-16

40

Pray for a Ceiling Garden

A friend told me about the garden she had on the ceiling of her childhood bedroom. Maybe you need to grow one for your daughter.

At the age of seven, Becky couldn't be sure if God was real. One parent believed in God and one didn't, leaving her a bit stuck. After she confided in her mom, together they opened the Bible to Jeremiah 29. The prophet Jeremiah was writing to the people of Judah during their exile under Nebuchadnezzar. Jeremiah was encouraging them to face a tough decision with hope and keep moving ahead with their lives:

> *"I know the plans I have for you," declares the Lord, "plans to prosper you and not to harm you, plans to give you hope and a future. Then you will call on me and come and pray to me, and I will listen to you. You will seek me and find me when you seek me with all your heart. I will be found by you," declares the Lord, "and will bring you back from captivity" (Jeremiah 29:11-14).*

The middle verse in that passage caught Becky's attention. She knew she had been looking for God with half of her heart. She decided to trust, seek, and pray with her whole heart.

Becky doesn't remember whose idea it was, but together she and her mom decided to track her prayer requests. (It was probably one of those times a parent leads a child along so they think it's their own idea, but really it came out of a pretty clear leading from mom.) The mom and daughter began to write down prayer requests on paper flowers and stick them on the closet door. When a prayer request was answered, they moved the flower to the ceiling where she could read and reread them. After just a few weeks, the ceiling garden had grown to more than 20 flowers, including one that read, "I want to know you more."

So do you want your daughter to grow spiritually? Try planting and nurturing a garden on her bedroom ceiling. If you have a son, maybe go with stars or footballs. If you have an older teenager who doesn't want mom or dad decorating their room, suggest they keep a prayer journal.

But always make sure one of those early prayer requests is the same as seven-year-old Becky: "I want to know you more." *

Prayer for Answered Prayer

Heavenly Father. We know you love us. We know you have great plans for every member of this family. We trust you know what's best. Put your will at the center of Hailey's heart, so her prayers are at the center of your heart. Give Hailey a room and life filled with answered prayer. All to your glory. I pray this and all things in the name of your Son, Jesus. Amen.

"If you remain in me and my words remain in you, ask whatever you wish, and it will be done for you."

Jesus, in John 15:7

---

* Adapted from Nancy Sebastian Meyer, *Spiritually Single Moms* (Colorado Springs: NavPress, 2007), p.66.

41

Pray Despite the Pain

I'm thinking of 11 families in my circle.

I'm not going to name them, but I would describe them as solid Christian families who are plugged into Bible-believing churches and intentional about their faith. Most are intact families with a mom and dad who have stuck it out through thick and thin. Three of these homes are headed by a single parent who most assuredly provides his or her kids with love, consistency, and spiritual guidance.

In some cases I know the entire family. In other cases, I know just one of the parents. I've been in a small group with the men leading some of these families. The list also includes old neighbors, college classmates, work colleagues, and ministry partners.

You get the point. These are families very much like the ones in your circle. Well, in each of these 11 families, one or two of the kids are making or have made some bad choices.

You can guess the issues I'm talking about. Drugs. Runaways. Dropouts. Teenage pregnancy. Abortion. Alcoholism. Cults. Belligerence toward organized religion. Shoplifting. Identity theft. Total breakdown in communication with mom and dad.

In all 11 of these families, the parents spent time trying to fix the problem. They sought wise counsel. They joined support groups. Some spent significant amounts of money in the process.

Looking back, some parents can pinpoint the moment when they "lost" their child. Some saw it coming. Others were totally taken by surprise. In most cases, it was a slippery slope that started with something small and rapidly went downhill.

In every case, they haven't given up. In every case, they continue to pray hard. And that's the main takeaway from this chapter. Keep praying, Mom. Keep praying, Dad. God cares and he can draw your child back to you.

There are parallel lessons too. You are not alone. Lots of families go through this. Don't blame your spouse. Even if you don't agree on how to respond to the challenge, rally and come together to work toward the same goal. If you can see a potential problem coming, try to address it early. Also, don't abandon or ignore your other kids in the process.

You've heard this before, but please take it to heart. Young people sometimes make terrible choices, and a mother or father beating themselves up makes the situation worse, not better. Please, please, don't let it destroy your marriage.

Do I know of only 11 families going through this kind of struggle? Probably not. The fact is that we all likely know mothers and fathers from dozens of families who are going through the agony of a wayward son or daughter.

Some hide it. Some share it with their closest friends. Some are in denial.

For all those families. For your family. For my family. Let's pray.

Prayer for the Parents of Wayward Children

Heavenly Father. There's a lot of pain out there. Parents who think back to holding that newborn and imagining a wonderful future. And now they're being crushed by guilt, regrets, fear, judgment, and loneliness. We pray for those parents. They're on their knees praying every day for their lost children. Please hold them close. Give them hope. Give peace to their hearts. If you want them to take bold or drastic action on behalf of those kids they love so much, give them clear guidance. If you want them to wait patiently and trust in you, give them courage and endurance. Protect their marriages and families. And we join our prayers with the prayers of those hurting parents. Bring healing. Bring courage. Bring those kids back home. In Jesus' name. Amen.

Whoever fears the Lord has a secure fortress,
and for their children it will be a refuge.

Proverbs 14:26

42

Pray for Your Neighbors

Their dog digs up your rosebushes. Their teenagers play raucous heavy metal at 2 a.m. They have a rusted-out pickup parked on the edge of your property line. Their trees drip sap on the hood of your car.

Congratulations. You have just been given a wonderful opportunity to model authentic faith in action for your kids.

It's a two-step process. Two separate steps. Two steps that shouldn't overlap at all.

First, deal with it in a neighborly Christian way. Options include ways like these: On a nice, summer day when you're both outside trimming hedges or getting your mail, stroll over, compliment her garden gnome or the color of her front door, and then add an "oh, by the way." Which could be, "By the way, Donald saw your dog digging around his rosebushes. I wouldn't mention it except it happened a couple times, and Don loves his rosebushes. I thought you'd want to know."

Another "by the way" might go like this: "Hey, is that old Chevy for sale? I have a friend who restores old cars. And I can ask him what it might be worth. You may be sitting on a gold mine here. Did you have plans for it?"

A nice friendly conversation is a pretty good option. Probably don't call the cops on your neighbor or pound on his door in the middle of the night. Don't shoot the dog. Don't leave anonymous hate-filled notes. See if you can approach them in a nice way at the right time.

Second, pray about the situation yourself, asking God to intervene.
God really does care about your rosebushes, your sleep, and your witness to your neighbor.

But don't pray about your neighbor's irritating habit or disposition together with your kids. Instead, simply pray for their prosperity, health, and well-being. Pray for your own role as a great neighbor and witness. Because of telltale conversations around the house, your kids will know there's some frustration going on with the family next door. When you only pray good things for that neighbor, your kids will be left thinking you are the most grace-filled person in the world.

Your benevolent prayers—not even mentioning the dog, loud music, rusty truck, or tree sap—are actually part of the redemptive process. You know very well if you start praying about "how to make the problem go away," then your prayers will start to be judgmental and selfish. That's not prayer, that's venting. Instead, pray about what loving response God has for you to enact.

Always remember prayer time with your children is a chance to model authentic faith. Absolutely, you are in communication with the Creator. But you're also a parent 24/7 and your kids are watching.

By the way, if we really want to have a spiritual impact on our neighbors, we should do our best to keep our own dogs leashed, keep our own teens respectful, and keep our own yards tidy. When we fail, we need to be the first to ask forgiveness and work the hardest to change our ways. Our witness depends on it.

Mom and Dad, your neighbor may be your best pal with zero flaws. Or he may cause you occasional minor frustration. Or he may be the biggest jerk in town. No matter what, when you pray with your kids, be positive. Pray God into your neighbor's life. Pray for your own positive impact across the entire neighborhood. And pray that your children do the same.

Prayer for the Street Where You Live

Heavenly Father. You put us in this neighborhood. You gave us these neighbors. I would ask you to reveal your plan, but you already have. We are to love them. Jesus said, "We are to love our neighbor as ourselves." We are to live in such way that our neighbors ask what makes us tick—why we are so gracious, why we are so generous. And then you want us to respond in humility that we are just trying to reflect Jesus. To be his hands and feet. Really, we know what we have to do up and down our street. Help us to be the kind of neighbor you want us to be. In Jesus' name. Amen.

We who are strong ought to bear with the failings of the weak and not to please ourselves. Each of us should please our neighbors for their good, to build them up.

Romans 15:1-2

43

Pray Scripture

When my bride, Rita, moves furniture around every three or four months, I don't notice until I bang my shin, forehead, or hip on a table, lamp, or sideboard that wasn't there last time I looked.

I also don't notice fresh cut flowers. Not long ago, I stumbled down to the breakfast table and chirped, "These are lovely. Where'd they come from?" Rita looked up from her newspaper, rolled her eyes ever so slightly, and said, "They're left over from Kaitlin's shower. And they've been sitting on this table for…eight days."

For several years, I also didn't notice the five scripture verses posted on the side of the refrigerator. When I finally did notice them, I gave them a cursory once-over and didn't give it much additional thought. I assumed they were some holdover memory verses from one of Rita's long-ago women's Bible studies.

Then one day, I stumbled into the kitchen (again) and found Rita, eyes closed, leaning against the counter just inches from that short list of Bible verses. The thoughtful husband in me asked, "You okay?" "Yeah, just praying my verses for the kids." My hesitant reply was a simple, "Oh."

Well, it turns out that for years—and years—Rita had been praying specific verses of Scripture for each of our kids. God had given them to her. And she dutifully followed through.

If you're curious—and I hope you are—these are the five verses

Rita customized, paraphrased, printed off, posted on the fridge—and prayed for Alec, Randall, Max, Isaac, and Rae Anne just about every day while they were growing up in our house.

> I pray that Alec does not forget you, the Lord his God, by not keeping your commandments, your judgments, and your statutes which you command him today. I pray that he shall remember the Lord his God, for it is you who give him the power to be successful (Deuteronomy 8:11,18, paraphrased).

> I pray that Randy will remember whatever things are true, whatever thing are noble, whatever things are just, whatever things are lovely, whatever things are of good report, if there is any virtue and if there is anything praiseworthy—that he will meditate on these things (Philippians 4:8, paraphrased).

> I pray that Max will wait on you, Lord, and that he shall renew his strength. I pray that he shall run and not be weary, and that he shall walk and not faint (Isaiah 40:31, paraphrased).

> I pray, Lord Jesus, that if Isaac abides in you and your words abide in him, he will ask what he desires, and it shall be done for him (John 15:7, paraphrased).

> I pray that Rae Anne will not be conformed to this world, but that she will be transformed by the renewing of her mind, that she may prove what is the good and acceptable and perfect will of God (Romans 12:2, paraphrased).

If you happen to know our kids, you know that these verses touch at the very heart of who they are and reflect God's strategy for how he hopes to use them to bring glory to himself.

I totally recommend you ask him to give you a verse or two for each of your children. Feel free to steal one of the verses Rita has been praying for our kids. A better idea might be to meditate on each child.

Who they are. Their gifts. Their struggles. Their dreams. Then turn to your favorite Bible app or reference book and see if God leads you to one particular portion of Scripture for each of your kids that fits exactly right.

Post it someplace conspicuous and see if your loving and observant spouse notices. If your kids see it, that's okay too. When a child knows they are getting prayed for by a parent, that's a good thing.

Prayer for the Word to Work

Heavenly Father. Thank you for the gift of the Bible. Sometimes we think of it as just a book of instructions. Or history. Or prophecy. But it's so much more. It's you speaking to us. It's a living picture of your holiness. It's Jesus. It's a prayer you gave us so that we can give it back to you. Please write my children's names in every passage of your book, and inscribe them permanently in your book of life. We love and trust you. In Jesus' name. Amen.

All Scripture is God-breathed and is useful for teaching, rebuking, correcting and training in righteousness, so that the servant of God may be thoroughly equipped for every good work.

2 Timothy 3:16-17

44

Pray for Their Teen Years

If your son or daughter is approaching the teen years, a cynical world says you should be very, very afraid. At 12 years, 364 days your little angel will still be a little angel. But pessimistic parents of older children will sardonically warn that one day later, when they blow out 13 candles, they instantly morph into some kind of flesh-eating zombie.

Don't believe it. Don't repel your teen with negative expectations. (Expectations often become self-fulfilling prophecies.) Instead, stay positive. Keep doing what you're doing. You may have to reevaluate some of your methods of communication and discipline, but the strategy is the same.

- *You still need to enter their world.* Until now, that was easy because it was a world you created. Now they live in a world you may not understand or appreciate because it's one they've created with friends and influences that aren't on your radar.

- *You still need to spend time together.* At one time, they would eagerly drop everything on their schedule to make time for you. Now you may have to adjust your schedule to make time for them. That may mean talking after midnight, scheduling a weekly breakfast date, or taking a long weekend to escort them to a basketball tournament, dance recital, wilderness expedition, college visitation, or science fair.

- *You still need to express your love to them.* Now with their multitude of distractions, they might not always hear you. And if they do hear you, they might not always say it back. Plus, they're adding new definitions to the word *love* that scare you a little.

I submit that parents with teenagers should keep their expectations high. Seeing your little boy or girl discover, engage, and develop their gifts is quite satisfying. It's especially wondrous when they start doing things that you never dreamed of doing yourself.

All that to say, your teenager is in transition. And so are you. When Rae Anne boxed up her American Girl collection, it was heartbreaking. When Alec quit wrestling after his sophomore year, I took it hard. When a teenager drops something they've been doing for years and takes up with something that's outside your comfort zone, that's traumatic for any parent. To your teen it may have been the hardest decision of their life or maybe "no big deal."

Specifically, here are six things you need to pray—not for them, but for *yourself*—while you endure the changing world of your child's adolescence.

1. *Pray for a discerning memory.* You may be overwhelmed at the frightening memories of the poor choices you made as a youth. That's a valid concern. But your kids are not you. And somehow you lived to tell the tale. Pray for your kids also to make mistakes—small ones. And pray for a very quick learning curve.

2. *Pray for stoicism.* As a wise veteran of life, you see obstacles and roadblocks that will throw your teenager off track. Your entire being—down to your toes—tells you to shout a warning and prevent them from taking a single wrong step. But maybe the best choice is to let them take that step and see where it goes.

3. *Pray for patience.* They will grow up, but it takes awhile. Later, you'll look back and be amazed at how quickly it flashed by.

4. *Pray for the wisdom to know when to intervene.* Sometimes your teenager needs to be prodded. Or stirred. Or rescued. The slippery slope is sometimes more like a precipice. You'll want to catch them before they go over the edge.

5. *Pray that your idea of success does not prevail.* For your kids, you want fame, fortune, a loving spouse, and a long, healthy life. Well, guess what? It may be hard to take, but God may have other plans.

6. *Pray for their friendship.* A lot of experts say parents shouldn't be friends with their kids. And I get that. You're the authority figure. Your adult influence can be what keeps them from making wrong decisions. But you should also be able to enjoy your time with them. To laugh, talk, and learn from each other. That's the goal on the other side of the teenage years.

Stay connected. Expect good things. Pray. And don't worry so much. Hey, they're just kids. How much trouble can teenagers really get into? (Yikes.)

Prayer for Who They Are

Heavenly Father. You made young people in your image too. And as they try to figure it all out, they are going to make all kinds of choices. And it seems like every generation has a new set of challenges and temptations. Lord, reveal to them who you are and how you're the answer to all their questions. You are truth, love, and justice. You are peace and purpose. We love Lauren, Luke, and Connor for who they are. Make them yours, Lord. Make them yours. We pray for a surrendered life for these young people and our role as parents. In the name of your Son, Jesus. Amen.

Blessed are all who fear the LORD,
who walk in obedience to him...
your children will be like olive shoots
around your table.

Psalm 128:1,3b

45

Pray Conspicuously

The Payleitner family prays in restaurants. Whether it's just Rita and me. Or all 13 of us. We grasp hands around the table. Very few words are spoken. It all takes less than 20 seconds. People at the next table would probably not even decipher any of the actual words that are spoken. But anyone watching would know what just happened. The words might be as simple as "Thank you, Lord. We love you. In Jesus' name. Amen."

Is it for show? Of course not. It's to thank God, remind my family of his provision, and give him glory.

But on second thought, I guess it is part of a public demonstration. It's a statement of faith for all to see. And that's happening less and less these days. As head of the family, I take care to not make any fanfare at all. But part of me hopes my family's small gesture is an encouragement to anyone who might notice.

I have to think that occasionally at a restaurant, people have taken notice and thought, *Huh, I guess faith is alive and well in some families.* Of course, it's up to those of us at the table to refrain from throwing food across the room, cursing the overcooked pork chops, pinching the waitress, or engaging in any other hooliganism. The last thing we want to do is cast Christians in a negative light.

My kids and I have talked about that. If you let folks dining or working in a restaurant know you're a Christian, you have to tip well, and you can't squeal your tires leaving the parking lot. In your neighborhood, if you have presented yourself as a home where Christ is the central figure, you really can't let your dandelions spread to your neighbor's lawn, play basketball in your driveway past 10 p.m., or curse at your dog when he runs out the front door with your slipper in his mouth.

The same principles apply on the job. If we occasionally read our Bible over lunch, we're making a statement *and* becoming a potential target. Our colleagues should see us as the kind of person who won't steal office supplies, stab someone in the back, gossip, or fudge expense reports. They may even come to us for advice, share a personal problem, or ask for prayer.

Most of the people passing through your life should quickly come to realize that your family puts God first. That includes friends, extended family members, work colleagues, neighbors, and the parents of the children with whom your kids go to school or play sports. And—no pressure—but your life should be a shining example of faith.

> *"You are the light of the world. A town built on a hill cannot*
> *be hidden. Neither do people light a lamp and put it under*
> *a bowl. Instead they put it on its stand, and it gives light to*
> *everyone in the house. In the same way, let your light shine*
> *before others, that they may see your good deeds and glorify*
> *your Father in heaven" (Jesus, in Matthew 5:14-16).*

On first reading, you might think this passage is about you. "You are the light." "Your light shines." "Your good deeds." It's *your* faith that needs to light the way. Visible. Attractive. Open and obvious to the world. That's something your children definitely need to see. But the last phrase brings it home. It's all to "glorify your Father in heaven."

You and your children have a responsibility to draw people to the light of Christ. False religions and worldly entanglements can shine deceptively bright, but they are not lighthouses guiding home lost souls. Those deceptive, destructive lights might best be described as human bug-zappers.

Mom and Dad, think of your faith as a beacon that brings

truth-revealing light to the world. Your conspicuous God-honoring life can impact your neighbors, coworkers, and community. That same light may also lead your children home and warn them about the crashing waves and rocks as they navigate through life.

Prayer to Be Salt and Light

Heavenly Father. Help my family reflect your values and your truth in all we do. Help us have an attractive faith. Not showy. Not for our glory. But for yours. When people see our attitude and love, my prayer is that they see something valuable and authentic. Something they want to have for themselves. Help every member of our family be a living example of your love. I pray this in the name of your Son, Jesus. Amen.

"By this everyone will know that you are my disciples, if you love one another."

Jesus, in John 13:35

46

Pray Briefly

Can you pray too long? According to a dear friend, *yes*.

Several years ago over lunch I was surprised to hear he was thinking about quitting our church drama team. At least two or three times per month, his presence added much to the sketches and dramatic vignettes during our weekend service. The original pieces were remarkable and creative. The variety was endless. Slice-of-life dramas. Slapstick. Soliloquies. Audience interaction. Situation comedies. Musical theater. Pantomime. Parodies. Newscasts.

Over pub burgers, he explained how the volunteer actors received scripts on Mondays and rehearsed on Thursdays. It was clearly a lot of work, but they had fun and their efforts were appreciated. My friend, a busy father and business professional, committed to stay as long as necessary on those Thursday nights until they got it right. And, he told me…"We spend way too much time in prayer."

Yikes. Did I hear that right?

My friend was a devoted Christian and spiritual mentor to me. He knew the value of prayer. He would be the first to acknowledge that any worship service is meaningless without divine guidance. Even the most eloquent sermon falls on deaf ears unless the Holy Spirit opens the heart of people in the pew.

He explained how the director and cast for that week's drama would meet at 7 p.m. for rehearsal and open in a small prayer circle. Which is a wonderful thing. But often 40 minutes later they were still praying.

In frustration, my friend confessed—after eight or ten minutes—his mind went elsewhere. He had questions about the script. He was thinking about all the blocking they had to do. And character development. And comic timing that had to be worked out. And he was hoping to still get home to tuck his kids into bed.

If there was something out of the ordinary going on or someone had a personal issue to work through, he totally understood. He would be the first to offer sincere, heartfelt, and sometimes extended prayer. But that wasn't typically the case. In his own words, the group prayer tended to be "repetitive, redundant, and repetitively redundant."

My friend felt guilty about his adverse response to that prayer circle. Until now, he never mentioned this to anyone but his wife. He never whined to the director or polled the other actors.

As he presented his thoughts over lunch, I had to agree with him. Although I encouraged him to talk to the director or head of the drama ministry.

Thinking about it later, I recalled being in similar situations myself. But they were single occasions. A ministry group had gathered for a specific task, or maybe it was at the close of an already-long church meeting, and it seemed like some of the pray-ers liked the sound of their own voices. They went on and on and on. I've also witnessed a large-group dynamic in which it felt like a competition over who could pray longer and with more sincerity.

Have you been there? Can you relate?

Still, maybe my friend and I are both wrong. Maybe it's impossible to pray too long. After all, Paul told us to "pray without ceasing" (1 Thessalonians 5:17 NASB). Never ceasing is a long, long time. But I don't think he was talking about living on your knees. He was calling believers to seek continual connection to God and acknowledging our dependence on him. That kind of prayer can happen *while* you're rehearsing a scene, giving a sales presentation, or kneading bread dough, right?

My friend's point was this: God knows why the drama team is there. He already knows exactly what every performer needs. So why not give thanks, give glory, put in your request, and get to work? It might even be a matter of good stewardship. We all only have so much time in the day—let's use it wisely.

As you read some of the psalms, it may seem like God likes long prayers. But there's quite a bit of biblical support suggesting that length is not the best way to judge prayers.

> *Do not be quick with your mouth,*
> *do not be hasty in your heart*
> *to utter anything before God.*
> *God is in heaven*
> *and you are on earth,*
> *so let your words be few.*
> *A dream comes when there are many cares,*
> *and many words mark the speech of a fool.*
> *When you make a vow to God, do not delay to fulfill it. He has*
> *no pleasure in fools; fulfill your vow. It is better not to make*
> *a vow than to make one and not fulfill it (Ecclesiastes 5:2-5).*

In that passage, Solomon seems to be saying that God wants you to think before you speak, make your point, and then keep your promise. We might even call it "prayer efficiency." Then there are Jesus' instructions about prayer in the Sermon on the Mount.

> *"When you pray, do not keep on babbling like pagans, for they*
> *think they will be heard because of their many words" (Mat-*
> *thew 6:7).*

The Bible provides several examples of short, powerful prayer. In an earlier chapter we took a longer look at Luke, chapter 18, when Jesus compares the boastful prayers of a Pharisee with the humble prayer of a heartbroken tax collector. It's an example of an awesomely perfect prayer that is only seven words long.

> *"The tax collector stood at a distance. He would not even look*
> *up to heaven, but beat his breast and said, 'God, have mercy*
> *on me, a sinner'" (Luke 18:13).*

Three final thoughts. First, with your kids, don't be afraid to pray short. Or long. Or whatever it takes. But do watch for signs of boredom.

Second, if your children say a two-second prayer on the way out the door, that's fantastic. If you happen to catch them on another occasion praying from the heart for several minutes, even better.

Third, I apologize this chapter went so long. My original goal was to make this one of the shorter chapters in the book. But sometimes it really does take a while to say what needs to be said.

Prayer for Effective Prayer

Heavenly Father. Every time we turn to you is a victory. Help us to not judge prayer. In the name of your Son, Jesus. Amen.

"Watch and pray so that you will not fall into temptation. The spirit is willing, but the flesh is weak."

Jesus, in Matthew 26:41

47

Pray for a Parking Space—Or Not

My children razz me because sometimes I'll pray—right out loud—for a parking place. My daughter insists that God shouldn't be bothered with such trivial matters. Or that I shouldn't make such a selfish prayer. Or that if I'm talking to God, I should talk about things that really matter. Or that the bigger picture of God's plan probably does not depend on me snagging a parking spot right next to the burger joint.

She makes some excellent points. I really can't disagree with her. But I do anyway.

I love getting in theological debates with my children. When Rae Anne jabs me for praying for a parking spot, for nice weather for a picnic, or to find my car keys, I can respond with solid biblical support.

I might say, "Hey, you know God wants us to go to him in every situation," and I would back that up by quoting Philippians 4:6.

> *Do not be anxious about anything, but in every situation, by prayer and petition, with thanksgiving, present your requests to God.*

Rae Anne might respond, "Sure, Dad, we can go to God anytime for anything. But that verse is about anxiety. God wants us to turn our worries into prayers. If you were racing to the hospital because I was in a car accident and you were all stressed over where to park, sure go ahead and pray for your parking space. But otherwise..."

Then I might say, "Sweet daughter, but God cares about the tiniest details of our lives," and then I might quote Matthew 10:30: "Even the very hairs of your head are all numbered."

Rae Anne might respond with something like, "You're right, Dad, God knows everything about you. He knows exactly how many hairs were on your head yesterday and exactly how many fewer hairs are on your head today. God absolutely knows the instant you begin looking for a place to park. But if it doesn't impact your life or someone else's life, why would you even consider asking him for help?"

Then I might say, "God has the power to do anything!" and quote Luke 1:37: "Nothing is impossible with God (NLT)."

Rae Anne might say, "Really, Dad? When you've got the attention of the Creator of the universe, the most crucial thing you are going to ask of him is to find you a place to park your Ford Escape? I gotta tell you, Dad—that's a little sad."

Like I said, I love kicking around theological questions with my kids. Especially the slightly opinionated and occasionally sarcastic Rae Anne. Maybe you're thinking that she should submit more to my authority, but every conversation has a foundation in love, respect, and unequivocal commitment to each other's best interest. I want all my children to think for themselves and sharpen their skills at defending their faith and beliefs.

Just between you and me, I'm not sure if it's a good idea to pray for a parking space. It does seem like one of those trivial prayers that only an upscale American might make. And I certainly don't want to be one of those people who find an opening right in front of the bagel shop and cry, "God, you are so good!" I am pretty sure God is good even if I have to circle the block a few times before finding a space.

On the other hand, if I'm "praying continually" as instructed in 1 Thessalonians 5:17, then shouldn't I mention my simple and immediate need as I approach my destination? My prayer does not pull God away from more critical prayers made by those who are starving, suffering, or facing persecution. I'm simply acknowledging that he is in control of all things at all times.

Reading all the above, you might be thinking, *Jay, what does this have to do with me and my two toddlers?* Well, probably not too much. It may be more than a decade before you want to hold a conversation or debate with your kids over these kinds of head-scratching issues. But you can and should begin praying now for them to have curious minds when it comes to God and how, when, and why we turn to him for all our needs.

One tangible application of this chapter might be this. Next trip to Target, Pottery Barn, or Goodwill, let your little ones hear you pray right out loud for a parking spot. Expect them to look out the window and shout, "There's one!" Your response is obvious: "Thanks, God."

Maybe I should have done that more often with Rae Anne.

Prayer with Older Kids

Heavenly Father. Thank you for this outing with David. It's a rare privilege. Help us find the right shelf unit for his dorm room without spending too much money, time, or gas. Be with us in our conversation. Help me listen and learn from him. And maybe the other way around as well. We love you. And we pray in Jesus' name. Amen.

I long to see you so that I may impart to you some spiritual gift to make you strong— that is, that you and I may be mutually encouraged by each other's faith.

Romans 1:11-12

48

Pray with a Paintball Gun

Raising three sons, a friend of mine knew the best way to get their attention when it came to devotionals or passing along theological truths was to set something on fire or blow something up. And it worked.

Tim Shoemaker is an accomplished author and speaker,* but deep down he's still a bit of science geek and a kid at heart. Which can be a great help when you're trying to connect with three curious boys. Once Tim put an egg in a microwave to demonstrate the danger of hidden sin. When the egg exploded after about 60 seconds, he pointed out how it looked perfectly fine on the outside, but something was churning and cooking on the inside. Sin—even if it takes a while—is going to blow up in your face.

Tim also dropped a dill pickle into a super-cold slush of crushed dry ice and acetone. After two minutes, he pulled the pickle out of the minus-100-degree solution and it was rock-solid. One whack with the hammer and the pickle smashed to pieces. Tim then talked about the prideful hearts of Pharaoh and King Nebuchadnezzar, as well as Proverbs 28:14, which promises, "Whoever hardens their heart falls into trouble."

When it comes to prayer, Tim knows that one of the challenges for young Christians is to keep praying even when you don't see any direct

---

* For information about one of Tim's resources for dads, see the back of this book.

answers. To make that point for his boys, Tim painted a sheet of plywood blue and then loaded up a couple paintball guns with blue pellets. The boys fired away at the plywood and the paintballs splattered nicely. But because the result was blue on blue, they really couldn't see any of those wonderfully satisfying splats. Tim told his boys, "Shooting a paintball gun is fun…but when you can't really see the results of how the paintballs hit the target…it loses something. The same thing can happen with prayer. We don't always see the answers to our prayers. When we can't see the results it's pretty easy to lose interest and to say 'why bother?'"[9]

In his book *Mashed Potatoes, Paint Balls and Other Indoor/Outdoor Devotionals You Can Do with Your Kids,* Tim describes how he followed up the paintball shooting with three reasons we need to pray even when we don't see any dramatic results right away:

- *Prayer focuses our attention on God.* It reminds us of how we need him.

- *Prayer focuses our requests.* "Why am I asking for this?" "Is it really something God would want?"

- *Prayer allows God to work in us.* Often he'll show me my heart isn't right. He ends up changing me. He prepares me for his answer—whatever it is.[10]

Now, I'm not recommending you blow up anything in your kitchen or run out and purchase a small arsenal of paintball guns. But…wait a second. I change my mind. Absolutely—if you can prevent your kids from harboring hidden sin or having prideful hearts, go for it. Explode that egg. Smash that pickle. If you can teach them to pray even when they're not seeing direct answers to their prayer, then invest in a paintball gun or two.

Now exploding, smashing, and shooting stuff may not be your style, and that's fine. But parenting still requires you to kick-start your creative spirit. Especially when it comes to prayer. Don't trivialize prayer or make a joke of it. But every parent should make it a point to mix it up sometimes. Pray on your knees. Pray on your treadmill. Pray long.

Pray short. Pray gardening. Pray playing tennis. Pray with the lights out. Pray in the sun. Pray surrounded by stuffed animals. Pray after building a church of Legos. Pray to be strong. Pray to be weak. Pray as if your life depended on it. Because it does.

Mom and Dad, please don't let prayer be boring. Hey! You're communicating with the Creator of the universe. And he's listening!

Prayer for Surprises

Heavenly Father. There is nothing boring about you. You are the Creator of butterflies and dandelions. And the creator of volcanoes and shooting stars. As parents, help us convey the excitement of knowing you to our kids. Help us be courageous enough to try some new ways to pray. And new ways to speak truth into the lives of these children you have given to us. And new ways to get closer to you ourselves. We pray this and all things in the name of your Son, Jesus. Amen.

ᆱ

"I tell you, whatever you ask for in prayer, believe that you have received it, and it will be yours."

Jesus, in Mark 11:24

49

Pray a Blessing

In the timeline of the New Testament, we first meet John the Baptist leaping for joy the first time he is in the presence of Jesus. That's Luke 1:41, when both happened to be babies in their mothers' wombs.

When we jump ahead in Matthew 3 to meet a grown-up John the Baptist preaching in the Desert of Judea, he's wearing a garment of camel hair, eating locusts and wild honey, and drawing quite a crowd. He's encouraging people to confess their sins and then baptizing them in the Jordan River. The Pharisees and Sadducees stop by to hassle John, and he responds with a passionate speech calling them all snakes and comparing them to fruit trees that don't produce fruit and clearly deserve to be cut down and burned.

His next statement to the crowd sets the stage for Jesus. John says,

> "I baptize you with water for repentance. But after me comes one who is more powerful than I, whose sandals I am not worthy to carry. He will baptize you with the Holy Spirit and fire" (Matthew 3:11).

Sure enough, just two verses later Jesus takes the first step in his three-year public ministry. He's about to spend 40 days being tempted in the desert and then handpick his twelve-man posse. But first he needs to get baptized and blessed by his Father.

Then Jesus came from Galilee to the Jordan to be baptized by

John. But John tried to deter him, saying, "I need to be bap-
tized by you, and do you come to me?" Jesus replied, "Let it be
so now; it is proper for us to do this to fulfill all righteousness."
Then John consented.

As soon as Jesus was baptized, he went up out of the water. At
that moment heaven was opened, and he saw the Spirit of God
descending like a dove and alighting on him. And a voice from
heaven said, "This is my Son, whom I love; with him I am well
pleased" (Matthew 3:13-17).

That's a pretty sweet model for how a parent can bless a child. "I love you without condition. My child, you bring me joy."

If you didn't notice, there's something really stunning about that blessing from God the Father to Jesus. Jesus had not yet begun his earthly ministry. He really had not done *anything* yet. Still the Father was "well pleased" with his Son. Is it possible that we too can tell our sons and daughters that we are proud of them even when they haven't done something awesome recently?

Mom. Dad. Do this with each of your kids. Bless them. Officially tell them you love them. No matter who they are or what they've accomplished. No matter what their teachers, coaches, friends, or grandparents say. Your kids are waiting for their mom and dad to tell them explicitly that they are worthy of love. With your child right there, turn to God and dedicate your son or daughter to his service and glory. Give your blessing. And ask for God's blessing.

Your official blessing could be a one-time event on their thirteenth birthday. Or maybe you pray over them every fall as you send them off to school. Or offer a blessing every night when you tuck them in.

I know parents who have orchestrated a significant "rite of passage" to mark their child's entry into adulthood and adult responsibility. You may want to present them with a token gift to mark the occasion: a ring, a Bible, a sword, a necklace, a letter, a set of car keys, or a pony. (Probably not a pony.)

If a one-time event sounds like something you want to initiate, don't hesitate. If you wait for the right moment or work out every detail, it may never happen. Pick a date on the calendar and give them a bless-ing. *Your* blessing. No excuses.

Day after day, we watch our little boys and girls grow, but one day soon we will turn around with amazement to see they have become men and women.

Prayer of Blessing

Heavenly Father. When Mackenzie entered this world, she was a blessing beyond belief. Every day since, my love for her has grown. The joy and happiness she brings our family is overwhelming. I love her more than words can say. I give her my blessing. It seems impossible, Lord, but I know you love her even more than I do! Continue to bless her and prepare a place for her in heaven. I pray in the name of your Son, Jesus, who—because of your love—you sent to the cross for Mackenzie and all man-kind. Amen.

[Jacob told Joseph], "Bring [your sons] to me so I may bless them"…

He blessed Joseph and said, "May the God before whom my fathers Abraham and Isaac walked faithfully, the God who has been my shepherd all my life to this day, the Angel who has delivered me from all harm— may he bless these boys. May they be called by my name and the names of my fathers Abraham and Isaac, and may they increase greatly on the earth."

Genesis 48:15-16

50

Pray During Commercials, on a Dirt Road, Tucking In, and over Waffles

In Deuteronomy, Moses gave instructions regarding very specific occasions during which parents should be intentional about impressing God's commandments on their children. Those occasions were not exclusive events or milestones. Moses was clearly stating that moms and dads should be pouring truth into the hearts and minds of their kids during the routine moments of life.

> These commandments that I give you today are to be on your hearts. Impress them on your children. Talk about them when you sit at home and when you walk along the road, when you lie down and when you get up (Deuteronomy 6:6-7).

With a little creative application for the twenty-first century, it's pretty easy to apply these verses to the relationship you have with your kids. It's a three-part strategy. *Enter their world. Talk about what's right in front of you. Connect it back to God.*

Tracking with those verses written in Moses' final days, let's see how that three-part strategy works. Moms and dads are instructed to anticipate four specific occasions:

When you sit at home. Next time your son or daughter is watching television, don't say, "Hey, why don't you turn that thing off and read a book or do something productive." Instead, plop down next to them and watch what they're watching. Then—not during crucial plot development—go ahead and ask them about the characters and their motivations. Or when a commercial comes on, talk about the message the advertiser is trying to convey. Don't judge every detail. But do connect what's on the screen back to God's design and his priorities for our lives. You probably won't do much praying while the TV is on, but you can make a spiritual connection. Of course, if they are sitting at home *not* glued to a screen you have an even better chance to have a conversation that leads to prayer.

When you walk along the road. On the next nice day, invite your son or daughter to take a walk. Don't get too deep or preachy because you want them to actually look forward to your *next* walk together. But do take advantage of the many opportunities to see God at work and respond with prayer. You're outside. Away from distractions. Cell phones are at home or stay in your pockets. Nature or neighbors are all around you. Treetops point to God. Cloud shapes prove his endless creativity. Quote Proverbs 6:6 when you see a row of ants: "Go to the ant, you sluggard; consider its ways and be wise!" When you pass a neighbor's house, pray for that family's children, their well-being, or their spiritual journey. And pray you and your family are a positive witness to everyone you meet. These principles for prayers on the road can also apply to all the traveling you do with your kids—by plane, train, or automobile.

When you lie down. This is not referring to your own nap in the middle of the day. This is all about tucking in the kids—kids of all ages. I'm a big fan of dads tucking in. Knowing that it's time to connect with Dad eliminates any whining about bedtime. You pray together for a good night's sleep and a good day tomorrow. But more than that, it's magic time when you're all safe at home and the crud of the day melts away. When the lights are dim and their head is on the pillow, your preschooler or teenager just might reveal experiences and thoughts you might otherwise never hear. At bedtime, you are actually *expected* to pray. So take full advantage.

When you get up. Before the busyness of the day, make it a point to lock eyes with each of your children. Speak encouragement into their day and into their life. If you know something specific going on, that's great. *"I'll be praying for your geometry test today." "You still have art on Tuesdays, right? I'm praying you have a blast." "I know the coach is working you hard before the tournament this weekend. At four o'clock, know that I'm praying for you and the whole team."* If you don't know what their day looks like, don't sweat it. Even a simple "Have a great day, son" is a connection that lasts. And, if you're fortunate to sit down for three minutes over grapefruit, bagels, or waffles, ask, "How can I pray for you today?" And then go ahead, right there, and make a heavenly connection.

Early and often every day. *Enter their world. Talk about what's right in front of you. Connect it back to God.*

Now go back and read those two verses from Deuteronomy again. You'll notice that before you impress, talk, sit, walk, lie down, or get up, parents are instructed to complete an important preliminary task. That's right. Mom and Dad, make sure the commandments God gives are first and foremost on *your* heart.

Prayer for Connected Lives

Heavenly Father. Life scatters families. But thankfully, you draw us together. Help me to be intentional about entering the world of my children so I can know and understand their hopes and dreams. Help me to know when and how to engage them in conversation. Or just to walk or sit beside them in comfortable silence. And always show me ways I can impress your truths into their lives. Oh yeah, help me know and embrace your truth in my own life. I pray this in the name of your Son, Jesus. Amen.

My people, hear my teaching;
listen to the words of my mouth.
I will open my mouth with a parable;
I will utter hidden things, things from of old—
things we have heard and known,
things our ancestors have told us.
We will not hide them from their descendants;
we will tell the next generation
the praiseworthy deeds of the LORD,
his power, and the wonders he has done.
He decreed statutes for Jacob
and established the law in Israel,
which he commanded our ancestors
to teach their children,
so the next generation would know them,
even the children yet to be born,
and they in turn would tell their children.

Psalm 78:1-6

51

Pray the Walls of Your Home

In the previous chapter, we kicked around four occasions during which we should "impress God's commandments on our children" on a daily basis. We read two verses in Deuteronomy that are all about being intentional during the routines of life.

> These commandments that I give you today are to be on your hearts. Impress them on your children. Talk about them when you sit at home and when you walk along the road, when you lie down and when you get up (Deuteronomy 6:6-7).

Well, the two verses that follow are not about specific times and places, but more about keeping strategic passages of God's promises right in front of you. Moses encourages parents to inscribe portions of God's laws on their doorways and gates, and even somehow carry them tied to their wrists or near their forehead as visual reminders.

> Tie them as symbols on your hands and bind them on your foreheads. Write them on the doorframes of your houses and on your gates (Deuteronomy 6:8-9).

Translating Old Testament instructions to the twenty-first century is sometimes tricky, but this doesn't seem too difficult or outrageous. Let's start with what Moses probably is *not* telling us today. Don't spray paint John 3:16 on your garage door. Don't rip out pages from your Bible and staple them to your forehead. And don't let your teenager tell you that Deuteronomy is commanding them to get a favorite Bible verse tattooed on their forearm.

Still, the idea of wearing scriptural truth as "symbols on your hands" might suggest a nice gold bracelet engraved with a favorite Scripture verse or even one of those stretchy wristbands that were so popular a few years back. A tasteful piece of jewelry or a fun wristband—why not?

At any rate, the idea of intentionally posting prayers or Scripture around your home is a really, really, really good idea. Without preaching, you're letting your kids, their friends, and any visitor know your family's priorities. Plus, you're holding yourself to the biblical standard as well.

For example, if you have Romans 12:18 framed in your living space proclaiming, "If it is possible, as far as it depends on you, live at peace with everyone," then supposedly there's a chance you might be a bit slower to anger. There are no guarantees—it's not magic—but I think that's fair to say.

With that in mind, let's take a stroll around Jay and Rita's house and see what we find.

In my office, biblical quotes are taped, nailed, and pushpinned all over the cluttered walls and bulletin board. My favorite is a small card with a graphic image that says, "See! I will not forget you...I have carved you on the palm of my hand. Isaiah 49:15."

Anyone walking in our front door immediately sees a graphic rendition of the Apostles' Creed by the well-loved calligrapher Tim Botts. Around the corner is a framed poster that asks, "What If He Is Who He Says He Is?" and the answer to that question is presented through 14 passages of scripture.

In our dining room is a favorite cross-stitch wrought by Rita with a farm scene and the block letters, "TO EVERYTHING THERE IS A SEASON, AND A TIME TO EVERY PURPOSE UNDER HEAVEN."

In the hallway upstairs, you can read Psalm 39:7—"LORD...my hope is in You"—and also John 8:12: "I am the light of the world."

In the back bedroom is the giant collage from my dad's memorial service. His granddaughters put it together and included one of his favorite notecards that features Philippians 1:3: "I thank God every time I remember you."

On the fridge are magnets that say, "With God All Things Are Possible (Mark 9:23)." Another one says, "Stop me before I volunteer again." But I don't think that's a quote from Scripture.

That's a brief overview of the Payleitner walls and other décor. Even a casual observer can't miss the idea that we think God is real and worthy of praise. I can think back on quite a few fascinating and rewarding conversations, debates, and heart-to-heart talks that have taken place in my home—conversations that started with a visitor noticing a poster, plaque, or piece of framed artwork. Many of which ended with a small group of us joined in prayer.

I would say, "If only these walls could talk." But it turns out, they can.

Prayer for Stuff We Can Do to Trigger Conversations

Heavenly Father. We know that Christian bumper stickers, T-shirts, and wristbands are not going to save the world. But we do want to be a little bolder in our witness. We want to know you more and tell others about you. Without going over the top or being offensive, help us stretch ourselves and be more public with our faith. And then give us the right words to say. I pray in the name of Jesus. Amen.

❧

It is the same with my word.
I send it out, and it always produces fruit.
It will accomplish all I want it to,
   and it will prosper everywhere I send it.

Isaiah 55:11 NLT

52

Pray for Their Salvation

I was jealous when our neighbor Joan led my oldest son, Alec, through the prayer during which he trusted Christ as his personal savior.

The summer before Alec began second grade, we moved to a new neighborhood. Joan's son, Paul, was in the same class and the two boys became best pals. That fall, Paul invited Alec to go to AWANA. Rita and I had checked out the church and the program, and we were glad for the connection. It wasn't our home church, but the weekly gatherings were well run and a great place for my son to spend Wednesday evenings.

Alec was quick to pick up on the competitive aspect of AWANA, and he progressed eagerly through the handbook, committing the core verses of the plan of salvation to memory:

- Romans 3:23. All have sinned and fall short of the glory of God.

- Romans 6:23. The wages of sin is death, but the gift of God is eternal life in Christ Jesus our Lord.

- Romans 5:8. God demonstrates his own love for us in this: While we were still sinners, Christ died for us.

- Titus 3:5. He saved us, not because of righteous things we had done, but because of his mercy.

- Acts 16:31. Believe in the Lord Jesus, and you will be saved.

- John 3:16. God so loved the world that he gave his one and only Son, that whoever believes in him shall not perish but have eternal life.

Using those verses as a foundation, Joan led Alec through a few simple questions and a prayer. Alec got it. And that night, my son became a true believer. Beginning a journey of growing faith here on earth. And secure in his eternal home in heaven.

When Joan dropped him off, he gave us the news. Rita and I were delighted. And a little surprised. And, as I mentioned, I was a little jealous that I wasn't there to be part of that life-changing moment.

That may sound a bit selfish. But I'm just being honest. I know what Alec experienced that night was cause for celebration. Angels cheer and high-five when a boy, girl, man, or woman receives Christ. Luke 15:10 describes the scene: "I tell you, there is rejoicing in the presence of the angels of God over one sinner who repents."

Thinking back, I guess I felt a little left out. Like arriving late to a party. So I offer that moment of mixed emotions as an insight for every parent with curious, eager, growing kids. Here are a few takeaways you may want to consider:

1. Know where your children are spiritually. Not interrogating them, but talking about how God loves us and explaining that knowing him means that our lives have meaning. He's going to make sure it all works out in the end.

2. Take them through those key Scripture verses above. Are they saying and memorizing a string of words? Or do they get the idea—the truth—behind those passages?

3. Sharp kids—like yours and mine—really can understand the simple, core truths of the gospel when they're in second or third grade.

4. Whether it's at your church or not, plug your kids into a regular gathering where caring adults share God's love and his story with your kids. I totally recommend AWANA. But there are other solid programs out there too.

5. Maybe volunteer yourself! That way, you'll be there for these life-changing moments for your kids. And their friends!

You'll be glad to know that Rita and I learned our lesson. Alec is our oldest. You can bet that Rita or I or both of us were there when Randall, Max, Isaac, and Rae Anne accepted Christ as their Savior.

Prayer for Their Deepest Need

Heavenly Father. This is not a prayer for Nathan to have a good day at school. Or make friends. Or become a doctor or lawyer. This is a prayer for Nate to seek you and find you. Please draw my son to you so he hears and understands his need for a Savior. Help him make that decision for himself. As soon as he understands, surround him with the right people and circumstances to be broken before you, accept your grace, and become your child. We pray in Jesus' name. Amen.

I tell you, now is the time of God's favor, now is the day of salvation.

2 Corinthians 6:2

Notes

1. Drawn from Jay Payleitner, *52 Things Kids Need from a Dad* (Eugene, OR: Harvest House Publishers, 2010), ch. 6.

2. Christian Answers.net, "The truth about angelic beings: What does the Bible really teach about angels?" http://christiananswers.net/q-acb/acb-t005.html.

3. Ron DiCianni, www.amazon.com/SPIRITUAL-Ron-DiCianni-Unsigned-Lithograph/dp/B001K28ZVI/ref=sr_1_1?ie=UTF8&qid=1402538093&sr=8-1&keywords=ron+dicianni+spiritual+warfare.

4. Nancy Guthrie, "Prayers That Move the Heart of God," *Today's Christian Woman,* March 2006, www.todayschristianwoman.com/articles/2006/march/9.22a.html?start=3.

5. Guthrie.

6. Jon Acuff, "Having a big fight right before church," Stuff Christians Like website, http://stuffchristianslike.net/2010/05/03/2961/.

7. Philip Yancey, "When Prayer Isn't Polite," www.beliefnet.com/Faiths/Christianity/2007/01/When-Prayer-Isnt-Polite.aspx#is1fryDqe6IHMTGk.99.

8. DC Talk, *Jesus Freaks: Revolutionaries* (Grand Rapids, MI: Bethany House, 2014), p. 87.

9. Tim Shoemaker, *Mashed Potatoes, Paint Balls and Other Indoor/Outdoor Devotionals You Can Do with Your Kids* (Chicago: WingSpread Publishers, 2007), www.amazon.com/Mashed-Potatoes-Paint-Balls-Devotionals/dp/1600661351/ref=sr_1_11?s=books&ie=UTF8&qid=1404596473&sr=1-11.

10. Shoemaker.

Books by Jay Payleitner:

Once Upon a Tandem
The One Year Life Verse Devotional
52 Things Kids Need from a Dad
365 Ways to Say "I Love You" to Your Kids
52 Things Wives Need from Their Husbands
One-Minute Devotions for Dads
If God Gave Your Graduation Speech
52 Things Daughters Need from Their Dads
52 Things Husbands Need from Their Wives
If God Wrote Your Birthday Card
52 Things Sons Need from Their Dad
10 Conversations Kids Need to Have with Their Dad
52 Things to Pray for Your Kids

About the author. Jay Payleitner is a dad. But he pays his mortgage and feeds his family working as a freelance writer, ad man, motivational speaker, and radio producer with credits including *Josh McDowell Radio, WordPower, Jesus Freaks Radio,* and *Today's Father with Carey Casey.* Jay served as the Executive Director for the Illinois Fatherhood Initiative and is a featured writer and speaker for the National Center for Fathering. He is the author of the bestselling *52 Things Kids Need from a Dad, 365 Ways to Say "I Love You" to Your Kids,* and *The One Year Life Verse Devotional.* He is also the creator of "The Dad Manifesto." Jay and his high school sweetheart, Rita, have four sons, one daughter, and four daughters-in-law and live in St. Charles, Illinois. You can sign up for his biweekly email at jaypayleitner.com.

National Center for Fathering

Engaging fathers. Enriching lives.

The National Center for Fathering (NCF) is a nonprofit 501(c)(3) organization created in 1990 in response to the incredible social and economic impact of fatherlessness in America.

At the National Center for Fathering, we work to improve the lives of children and reverse the trends of fatherlessness by inspiring and equipping fathers, grandfathers, and father figures to be actively engaged in the life of *every* child.

We focus our work in four key areas:

Research. At the core of all the National Center's work is the Championship Fathering Profile. Developed by a team of researchers led by NCF's founder, Ken R. Canfield, PhD, this assessment tool helps men understand their strengths and opportunities as a father. NCF continues to partner with researchers and practitioners interested in expanding the knowledge base of the fathering field.

Training. NCF offers training through seminars, small groups, and training programs. We have reached over 80,000 fathers through our seminars and have equipped more than 1000 trainers to provide our research-based father training in their local communities.

Programs. NCF provides impactful and meaningful fathering programs that enrich the lives of fathers, children, and families. WATCH D.O.G.S. (Dads Of Great Students), our flagship program, is currently in 46 states, four countries, and more than 4000 schools. WATCH D.O.G.S. is a one-of-a-kind school-based father-involvement program that works to support education and safety.

Resources. Our website provides a wealth of free resources for dads in nearly every fathering situation, including new dads and granddads, divorced dads and stepfathers, adoptive dads and father figures. Dads who join our *Championship Fathering Team* receive a weekly e-mail full of timely and practical tips on fathering. We also have a daily radio program that features Carey Casey, our CEO, and airs on 350-plus stations. Listen to programs online or download podcasts at fathers .com/radio.

For more information, please visit www.fathers.com.

Make your commitment to Championship Fathering

Championship Fathering is an effort to change the culture for today's children and the children of coming generations. We're seeking to reach, teach, and unleash 6.5 million dads, creating a national movement of men who will commit to LOVE their children, COACH their children, MODEL for their children, ENCOURAGE other children, and ENLIST other dads to join the team. To make the Championship Fathering commitment, visit fathers.com/cf.

10 Conversations Kids Need to Have with Their Dad

There's so much you want your kids to know and understand. You just need to find the right openings. And most dads could also use a little help filling in the gaps.

Veteran dad Jay Payleitner comes alongside with fresh ideas, trusted research, and experienced perspectives to help you communicate those all-important life values that will help your kids thrive—values around issues like...

- *Excellence*: how your kids can hit home runs in life
- *Work*: how to guide them to rewarding work that matches their gifts
- *Integrity*: how they can be true to something *beyond* themselves
- *Love, sex, and marriage*: how to tell them what you need to tell them
- *Eternity*: how they can own their faith and live as friends of the Creator

Dad, you can walk confidently alongside your kids on the road of life, well prepared to prepare them well. *Great gift or men's group selection.*

52 Things Sons Need from Their Dads
What Fathers Can Do to Build a Lasting Relationship

Bestselling author Jay Payleitner, dad of four grown sons, gives you a bucketful of man-friendly ideas on building a father-son relationship that will last into eternity. By your life, your example, and a few well-chosen words you can...

- show your boy why it's good to be a guy
- demonstrate how to treat women well
- teach him to work hard, set lofty goals, and find joy in the quest
- generate a positive outcome from competition, digital media, and video games
- lead him to count on God for the strength and confidence to live a purposeful life

Jay's 52 quick-to-read chapters offer real-life strategies that will inspire you and your son to keep fighting the good fight—together and on the same side!

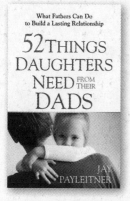

52 Things Daughters Need from Their Dads

What Fathers Can Do to Build a Lasting Relationship

The days of tea parties, stuffed doggies, and butterfly kisses are oh-so-important, but they don't last forever. So how can a dad safeguard his daughter so she grows up strong, healthy, beautiful, and confident?

Jay Payleitner guides you into what may be unexplored territory—*girl land*—and gives you ways to…

- date your daughter
- be on the lookout for "hero moments" and make lasting memories
- protect her from eating disorders and other cultural curses
- scare off the scoundrels and welcome the young men who might be worthy
- give your daughter a positive view of men

Jay will help you feel encouraged with 52 creative ideas to give you confidence in relating to your precious daughter…in ways that will help her blossom into the woman God has designed her to be.

Super Husband, Super Dad
You Can Be the Hero Your Family Needs
Tim Shoemaker

~~Faster than a speeding bullet!~~
~~More powerful than a locomotive!~~
~~Able to leap tall buildings in a single bound!~~
Treasures his wife and kids!
Asks for help when he needs it!
Does the right thing even when it's hard!

Every man desires to become the husband and dad God designed him to be. *Believe it or not*, an incredible marriage and parenting adventure is within your reach. Discover how to

- harness super strength to fight for your marriage
- perform death-defying feats while balancing time and resources
- knock out arch-villains like pride, complacency, and selfishness
- see through the walls of teenage rebellion
- reveal a not-so-secret identity rooted in Christ

Heroes wanted. The cape is optional.

The Awesome Book of Bible Answers for Kids

Josh McDowell and Kevin Johnson

These concise, welcoming answers include key Bible verses and explorations of topics that matter most to kids ages 8 to 12: God's love; right and wrong; Jesus, the Holy Spirit, and God's Word; different beliefs and religions; church, prayer, and sharing faith. Josh and Kevin look at questions like…

- How do I know God wants to be my friend?
- Are parts of the Bible make-believe, or is everything true?
- Was Jesus a wimp?
- Why do some Christians not act like Christians?
- Can God make bad things turn out okay?

The next time a child in your life asks a good question, this practical volume will give you helpful tips and conversation ideas so you can connect with them and offer straight talk about faith in Jesus. *Includes an easy-to-use learning and conversation guide.*